Dead Lines

Dead Lines

Slices of Life from the Obit Beat

George Hesselberg

WISCONSIN HISTORICAL SOCIETY PRESS

Published by the Wisconsin Historical Society Press
Publishers since 1855

The Wisconsin Historical Society helps people connect to the past by collecting, preserving, and sharing stories. Founded in 1846, the Society is one of the nation's finest historical institutions.

Join the Wisconsin Historical Society: wisconsinhistory.org/membership

The stories in this book were originally published in the *Wisconsin State Journal* and have been adapted for this collection.

Cover Photos: iStock.com/Rose_Carson; Scisetti Alfio/Shutterstock
Printed in the United States of America
Designed by Steve Biel Design

25 24 23 22 21   1 2 3 4 5

Library of Congress Cataloging-in-Publication Data

Names: Hesselberg, George, author.
Title: Dead lines : slices of life from the obit beat / George Hesselberg.
Other titles: Slices of life from the obit beat | Wisconsin State journal.

Description: Madison : Wisconsin Historical Society Press, 2021. | Includes index.
Identifiers: LCCN 2021025593 (print) | LCCN 2021025594 (ebook) | ISBN 9780870209666 (paperback) | ISBN 9780870209673 (ebook)
Subjects: LCSH: Madison (Wis.)—Biography. | Obituaries—Wisconsin—Madison. | Successful people—Madison—Wisconsin—Biography. | Poor people—Madison—Wisconsin—Biography. | Eccentrics and eccentricities—Wisconsin—Madison—Anecdotes. | Animals—Wisconsin—Madison—Biography. | Madison (Wis.)—Social Conditions—Anecdotes.
Classification: LCC F589.M153 A25 2021 (print) | LCC F589.M153 (ebook) | DDC 977.5/83—dc23
LC record available at https://lccn.loc.gov/2021025593
LC ebook record available at https://lccn.loc.gov/2021025594

Contents

Introduction

There are three deaths. The first is when the body ceases to function. The second is when the body is consigned to the grave. The third is that moment, sometime in the future, when your name is spoken for the last time.

—DAVID EAGLEMAN, NEUROSCIENTIST AND AUTHOR

I never really talked with George Bedessem until he was long dead. My first paying job was vacuuming old George's threadbare carpet in the living room of his tin-roofed house in the village of Bangor, Wisconsin, on Saturday mornings. He was in his eighties and paid me twenty five cents. I was seven or eight. He just showed me where to vacuum, and when I was finished, he would fish in his squeeze-open coin purse to find a quarter, and that was it. When I got my first hourly-paid job at fifteen, mowing the Fairview Cemetery, helping out with digging, and trimming around gravestones, I would always stop at his stone and have a chat.

Getting to know the dead didn't become a part of my life until I got my first daily newspaper job at the *Wisconsin State Journal* in 1972. I was part of a crew of college journalism students hired as interns for the summer. We did everything, including making beer runs for the night desk copy editors. The one thing we all did to start was to take obituaries over the telephone from funeral homes. This was in the days before paid obits, which are usually written by family members of the deceased.

We typed the obits on Remington typewriters, in duplicate with carbon paper. If a funeral director included some interesting bit of information about the person, we would bring it to the attention of Fred Curran, the night city editor, a tiny, courteous

1

man who drank beer from a small paper cup late at night. He would clear his throat and say to the chosen intern, "Why don't you give me a couple of 'graphs?" We would pray for the chance to add something beyond the routine and make a news story out of it.

Every editor I ever worked for on the city desk in those early days made it clear that a reporter has to respect the dead. In an obit, you get only one chance to get it right. The obit had to include certain information in a particular order and follow a certain style. Funerals were held "in" some place, but visitation was "at" some place. Spelling was sacred. After you typed the obit, you took an editing pencil and put editing marks throughout and drew a box around the name, which meant that the name's spelling had been double-checked. We also checked the morgue—the vast archive of news clippings—for past stories that might have mentioned the person.

An intern moved from taking obits to getting assignments to cover stories only if the obit initiation went well. Then the rookie began a rotation of shifts that usually still included obits but also city committee meetings, news briefs, and, if you were lucky, a move to the cop shop. Those obit beat skills took me down paths to some of my most interesting stories and all of the stories included here.

As a general assignment reporter, a crime reporter, and a columnist, I wrote about murders and mysterious deaths and the deaths that make the front pages. Many times, the circumstances of the death itself were what made it breaking news. It could have been a fatal fire, a traffic accident, a tornado, a flood. Other times it was the person who died making the story newsworthy: someone rich or famous or both. Those are good stories, too, but they are not in this collection. Those stories are about death. These stories are about life.

While working the police and fire beat. I started asking more questions about the lives of the people whose deaths would show up in the reports, simply labeled: "Death Investigation." I would read the police reports closely, looking for details that could be researched and confirmed, names of relatives, old jobs, curiosities. There was competition for stories, and I was looking for information no one else had or knew about or had tried to get. One key to a good story is in telling the readers something they didn't know. Finding that one little mystery might lead to an interesting story. Following this mantra became less a strategy than a habit. It helped me uncover stories that might not seem newsworthy—but that I thought were worth telling.

One night I came home from work, and my young son asked me, "Pops, did you write about anybody alive today?"

"No, not today."

But often I had written about a person's life.

In this book are stories about the people who populate the periphery of our own lives, contributing in a thousand unrecorded ways. Not all of these lives have happy endings. The temptation is great to tie everything up in a nice bow, but that is not the goal of a news obit. Here are quiet lives of inspiration, worthy of mention because of circumstance or because a detail may have jumped out and called for attention. Here are lives we may have always wondered about, mysteries (sometimes) solved, silences explained.

Mixed in are other tales, of immense sadness, of joyful memories, all connected in some way with the topic of death: missed pets, a beloved tarantula, a miracle survival. There are also a few stories about people and animals who were only thought to be dead: a cat who came back, a Vietnam vet who tried to hide, and a man who had to convince the government he was not dead. Like the others in this book, each of their stories provided the chance to reflect on a life and met my most important criteria for inclusion in this book: being a good read.

These stories were written between 1977 and 2017 for the *Wisconsin State Journal*, the daily newspaper in Madison, Wisconsin.

I accidentally started this book when I went into the archives to read a story I wrote when the peripatetic Cornelius Cooke died. I had mentioned him in a conversation with a friend about the characters in Madison. My favorites are the ones who would never consider themselves characters. Cornelius certainly didn't. Like several others in this collection, Cornelius was someone I tracked down while he was still alive. He was a familiar sight, but no one knew anything about him. So I just stopped one day and asked, and when he died, I revisited his story for an obit. The mystery was no longer in his appearance, but his disappearance.

It was a joy to read about Cornelius again, to remember the few times I had talked with him. I was grateful he shared his story, for the walnuts he kept in his pockets, and for the people who remembered him, who could help to fill in the blanks.

For the same reason, I looked up Angel Richardson, a woman with tiny bright dark eyes. She was not much taller than a fire hydrant, and she slowly walked the downtown streets of Madison for years. She wore a matted dark red wig and a thick shawl and dragged her bags along the sidewalk, from storefront to storefront and into the alcove outside the Memorial Library.

The pandemic caused the delay or cancellation of many funerals or get-togethers of friends and family. These events are where the stories are told, the acts of kindness and folly recalled, the memories of sacrifice and serendipity brought out one last time. Grudges are revealed and buried, missed opportunities recounted, romances relived, trophy bucks chased away, again. In their temporary absence, the importance of taking the time to pause and reflect became even more apparent. We must not hurry past these lives without noting the little things that set us apart from one another or pausing to appreciate what we all have in common.

An important part of the human experience is sharing it. I hope these stories remind others to do just that.

Lonely Missionary

Patricia Schoenrocker, 1913–1979

SEPTEMBER 30, 1979—Sister Pat is dead. Pray for her. She prayed for you.

Patricia Schoenrocker, care of General Delivery Baraboo, Middleton, Albany, Madison, and the Wisconsin Dells, died quietly Friday morning, probably of a heart attack. At 12:45 a.m. Friday, Capitol Police found the sixty-six-year-old Schoenrocker, a fixture of downtown Madison known for promoting her personal mission work, slumped over on a park bench at 10 West Mifflin Street. The bench had been her home, just as a grocery sack and the pockets of her five layers of clothing served as her office and bank. Her next of kin has not been found.

According to downtown observers, coroner investigator reports, and the items found in her grocery bag, Sister Pat had been one of the wandering, alley-haunting, parking ramp–camping street persons in Madison for some time.

Some years ago, she could be seen frequently around the Square, wearing her own makeshift version of a nun's habit. She drifted, panhandled, met and talked with various people, and frequently wrote rambling religious accounts of her meetings on whatever piece of paper was available. She then stuffed her writings into whatever pocket of clothing was nearest, crammed in with her money, buttons, bottle caps, keys, a wristwatch, scissors, and old letters. Some of the letters and various legal papers in her pockets were dated as far back as 1974.

"Every pocket of every piece of clothing she had on was filled with papers. Every piece of paper she ever came in contact with must have found its way into a pocket," coroner's investigator Philip Little said.

Dozens of tiny pieces of toilet paper, rolled up, were found. When those pieces of paper were unrolled, they contained money, bills. "There would be a few dollars stuffed here, another twenty dollar bill there," Little said. In all, investigators found $239.29 in cash in various pockets of a coat, two flower print dresses, a smock, and two T-shirts. There were twenty-six one-dollar bills, two five-dollar bills, eight ten-dollar bills and six twenty-dollar bills, alongside several mold-covered quarters, shiny dimes, and nine pennies.

Also in those pockets were savings account passbooks, all but one of the accounts closed. All had been in the name of the Interdenominational Mission, Sister Pat's self-designated church, of which she listed herself as president, vice president, and secretary treasurer on the accounts. Some of her writings also appeared to reference the Interdenominational Mission, referring to her "thirty-five years of mission work."

At a Baraboo bank, her savings account has $1,470, the last deposit recorded as December 15, 1978. She had $1,792.95 in her Wisconsin Dells bank when she closed that account in March 1978. All day Friday, investigators attempted to find a relative of Sister Pat. From papers in her pockets, they know she lived for a time at 425 East Johnson Street. Banks also were unable to provide more than an address of general delivery and a post office box number she once held in Middleton.

A circuit court commissioner late Friday appointed an attorney to handle her affairs. Her body was taken to Gunderson Funeral Home.

Nobody's Pet

Chief, 1972–1988

MARCH 15, 1988—Chief, a polar bear who never traded his dignity for a marshmallow, died at the Henry Vilas Zoo Sunday while being a polar bear.

Chief was shot by a police officer to save the life of a man who inexplicably jumped into Chief's spacious, unbarred pen. Acting on his natural response to a perceived threat, Chief mauled the intruder. The bear died, while the man who caused his death survived.

Monday morning a sprig of flowers was soaking in the snow in front of Chief's empty pen. A rock kept the card from blowing away. The card's handwritten message was, "We'll miss you, Chief. All your friends at the zoo."

Chief was born December 6, 1972, at the Jardin Zoologique du Quebec, Canada. By May 1973, Alvie Nelson, then director of the Henry Vilas Zoo, had applied to the National Marine Fisheries Service in the Department of Commerce for permission to import "one male polar bear" from Quebec. The cub was needed as a potential mate for a female polar bear, Nelson wrote, adding a polar bear had been in residence at the Madison zoo since the 1930s.

At eight months of age, the cub weighed 140 pounds and had already been named Chief.

Chief's file at the zoo does not mention how much he cost, but the records show he took two days to travel from Quebec to

Chief, pictured at Henry Vilas Zoo. ED STEIN, *WISCONSIN STATE JOURNAL*

Madison via Detroit in a truck driven by Dan Jackson. He arrived on January 28, 1974, a little more than a year old. His first diet here included daily doses of cod liver oil, cream, and vitamin E.

He was to grow and grow, becoming one of the largest polar bears in captivity. Though his baggy fur coat sometimes looked like droopy, fuzzy, white-yellow pajamas that flapped around his legs, Chief weighed between eight hundred and nine hundred pounds and was in excellent health. The only note about his health in the files was from 1980, when because of remodeling he stayed for a short while at the Milwaukee County Zoo. He had a nose cold, the file reported, and his daily diet then consisted of nine pounds of bread, four pounds of ground meat, two pounds of dog food, four pounds of fish, and a half of a head of lettuce. At home in Madison, his daily ration was a five-gallon pail of meat, chicken, and fish. Rick Bilkey, the education coordinator at the zoo who used to be the daily keeper of the bears, described Chief as "strictly a meat eater."

He had the company of a few female bears over the years, on loan from other zoos, and was listed in the world *Polar Bear Studbook*, but was alone these last few years. Zoo officials said the most recent den mate a few years ago had been an older female bear from the Lincoln Park Zoo.

Because of his size and uncompromising demeanor and because of the central location of his pen, Chief was the focal point of the zoo. While popular, he was nobody's pet. His keepers declined to describe his personality in human terms, instead speaking with respect for the powerful prowess of his species. "No one petted him, no one touched him," Bilkey said. "We all considered him the most dangerous animal here. He had no fear of man."

He was among the most difficult of the animals to keep or lure into his den. Once a week, when his pool was cleaned, he had to be locked into his den, but he was resistant to being lured in with treats, including marshmallows. "He didn't like it, and he knew when we were trying to get him to go in there. He was big enough to stay outside and stretch one leg into the den and scoop out some food," Bilkey said.

Chief was not much of a pacing animal. He would sit on his haunches, lolling in the sun, with eyes half-closed. He was big enough to be awesome even to adults, and his quick, silent movements could invoke fear. He was the most popular—and most photographed—in warm weather, when he would float or belly-flop, paws outstretched into his deep pool.

Bilkey spent a lot of time on the telephone Monday. Callers were making some strong statements about the bear, about the man who jumped into the den, and about the decision to shoot the bear.

Bilkey had to explain again and again that responders had no other choices, that this was not a situation for a slow-acting tranquilizer. Because the bear was responding naturally to an intruder and could easily have killed the man, the police officer had no choice but to shoot.

An effort to raise money to buy new polar bears will surely get a huge response. The incident also will likely lead to discussions about zoo security, about the appropriateness of keeping bears in a zoo, about how zoos used to be built to keep wild animals from the people, not the wild people from the animals.

Several taxidermists made offers Monday to stuff Chief, but the zoo declined their offers. That would have been the ultimate indignity to a polar bear born in captivity but never tamed.

A Second Chance in the Sun

Kenny Stout, 1925–1993

MAY 29, 1993—I met Kenny Stout and most of his twenty-two cats the day his mother died in December 1981, after she froze her legs in their unheated home in Verona. Kenny was fifty-seven at the time. He had noticed that his mother's legs were frozen and moved her from a cot to a chair to be closer to the coal stove, but that did not help. He called the ambulance from a neighbor's house on a Tuesday night, and she died in the hospital on Wednesday. Hypothermia was the cause. I learned this week Kenny died of a heart attack in Hawaii. The story of how he went from owning twenty-two cats and $1.83 in cash in 1981 to a grave in the National Memorial Cemetery of the Pacific in 1993 starts with his mother's death in that Nine Mound Road home.

Kenny had been a skinny, pleasant, unwashed man who took care of his mother the best he could. His appearance was remarkable only for a long nose wart he blamed on the cold weather. He was a familiar, if odd, sight in Verona, where he traveled around town on a bicycle outfitted with a homemade windscreen. In fact, he bicycled to the funeral home that December day to deliver his mother's best dress.

The death in 1981 exposed the circumstances of Kenny's life. He and his mother had lived in a one-story house filled with eighty years' worth of junk and garbage, almost two dozen cats, and a

Kenny Stout. L. ROGER TURNER, *WISCONSIN STATE JOURNAL*

single electrical outlet, into which Kenny plugged a hot plate and portable television set so his mother could watch Johnny Carson. The stove was so full of holes you could see the coals when the door was closed.

While grieving his mother, he was also worried about what would happen to him. At the time, he was not a candidate for a Happy Ending.

"I got a dollar eight-three left, and when that's gone, I guess I'll holler for help," he told me back then. "I guess in seven or ten days I'd like to head for California. I was there in the Navy. If that old car out there worked, and if I had a driver's license, I'd take seven or eight of the best cats and get out of here. I got some silver dollars I'm going to sell and go to California. I got some old pennies, too."

He and his mother were living off her $299 a month Social Security. Property taxes on the house had gone unpaid for four years. He was spending about seventy-five dollars a month at the grocery store, mostly on cat food, bread, and milk.

"I feed the cats bread soaked in milk," he said. "They all have names. I got one dead cat out in the yard. It's been too cold to bury it."

A year later, Kenny was still in Verona, but life had changed. The county's Community Action Commission weather-sealed his house well enough to give him one warm room for a time before he moved to a boarding house. A county social worker, Jo Sexton, arrived to help him get his life straightened out.

He sold some of his coins, got fifteen dollars for his lawn-mower, and twenty-five dollars for the 1961 Ford Fairlane that was rusting away alongside the house. An unidentified woman started showing up with cat food. She also gave him an electric blanket. The city offered assistance, but he turned it down.

An attorney appointed by the probate court found Kenny's long-dead father had left a tiny school pension. The house, a health and safety hazard, was bulldozed, and the lot sold for $20,500, which was used to pay back taxes and funeral expenses and other costs. He got the long wart removed from his nose.

After all that, Kenny ended up with about five thousand dollars and decided to go to Hawaii.

In December 1982, he sat in his room and read a March 12 issue of a Honolulu newspaper. In the Honolulu phone book, he looked up the names of friends he made in the Navy. He bought a bus ticket to Los Angeles and a plane ticket from there to Oahu.

On the way, though, the bus overturned in Nebraska and Kenny ended up in the hospital. The last I heard, he arrived in Hawaii in 1984 and had found a room.

Now comes word that Kenny died of a heart attack last January. His friends Kathy and Bill, who met Kenny after his troubles became public in 1981, wrote to say, "We'd like you to know that things turned out very well for Ken."

His obituary said that on Oahu, Kenny worked for the Honolulu Department of Parks and Recreation. He bicycled, walked the beach, wrote poems about Oahu, and "enjoyed his cats."

A Tidy Life

Harry Specht, 1936–1983

MAY 15, 1983—If you walked into Harry Specht's house at 1809 Elka Lane when he wasn't home, went down to the basement, over to a workbench, and moved a screwdriver an inch, he would know you had been there. That's the kind of guy he was: meticulous, orderly, with a place for everything.

A week ago Sunday, Specht tidied up his house before getting dressed in his best suit, vest, and polished black shoes. He put on a red tie and combed his hair. He made his bed, folded the weekend garbage into a sack, and placed it in the kitchen wastebasket.

Specht, forty-seven, was a quiet man. For the past sixteen years he worked as a water-meter repairman for the Madison Water Utility. Before that, he worked for the Forsberg Paper Box company for twelve years and put in one year on the Chicago and North Western Railroad. That about filled the years since he graduated from Madison Central High School in 1954.

"He kept pretty much to himself," his supervisor at the water utility said. "You might call him frugal, diligent, and not very social. If he had any close friends, it would surprise me. He avoided most of that kind of stuff. I guess he was kind of attached to his mother."

Last Sunday, before he went out to his car, Specht arranged his business papers in a neat row on the dining room table. Then he went to his car, a Ford Thunderbird, that was parked in the attached garage. He bought a Thunderbird every three years or so, from the same dealer, in Belleville.

To his car in the garage he took along his family's Christmas card registry, which lists the names of family and friends with their addresses. In a large envelope, he placed the obituary from his father's death in 1977 and the obituary from his mother's death in February. He included in the envelope a deed to a cemetery lot in the Sauk City Cemetery, a contract for the purchase of a gravestone from the Spellman Monument Company, and a business card from a trust officer at the M&I Bank.

He started the car and, with the garage doors shut and the car windows open, he was dead in a short time from asphyxiation. It was Wednesday when a police officer found Specht's body in the car, in the unlocked garage.

"The house looked like it was brand new on the inside," said an officer who was at the scene. "Even the cans of soup in the cupboards were lined up in neat rows, neater than in the supermarket."

In the envelope, authorities found a third obituary, this one handwritten by Specht, just as he wanted it published in the newspaper. He left "many cousins" as survivors. They also found, in the car, a Mother's Day card, signed by Specht. In the house, authorities found and took away for safekeeping what they have estimated to be more than five hundred thousand dollars' worth of jewelry, watches, and other valuables.

"He never threw money around, but he was generous to charities," a coworker said. "He was the same at work as he was at home, I guess. Everything had to be just so."

Everyone's Best Friend

Skipper, 1982–1990

NOVEMBER 27, 1990—Skipper, a golden retriever with a golden demeanor and ready nuzzle that made him a star with children, died Saturday of a heart attack.

The eight-year-old dog had been the unofficial Dane County Humane Society mascot, or "companion animal," as owner Jane Hanson described him. As outreach coordinator for the society, Hanson included Skipper in all of her activities. The genial Skipper was introduced to thousands of schoolchildren during Hanson's many speeches for the society.

"Skipper did a lot for kids who would have been terrified of a big dog," said Hanson.

Skipper—though docile, the wrong color, and definitely not afraid of humans—also played the part of wolf when Hanson gave talks about a specialty, wolves.

Changing roles was not unusual for Skipper. He wowed the media in September 1987 when he starred, cast as a female dog, in an advertising campaign on birth control for pets. He was also featured in newspaper, magazine, and other television advertising spots.

Hanson said Skipper had not been ill until a week before his death, when he had to be revived by mouth-to-mouth resuscitation (from Hanson's husband, Bill) after a heart attack. "He was doing fine, but when I took him out for a walk Saturday night, he just dropped over," Hanson said. "I'm a basket case over this."

Hanson purchased Skipper from a Watertown kennel. He started working with children when he was six months old, she said, and made his most recent public appearance two weeks ago.

His full name was Latasha's Klondike Skipper. He liked to sleep and, noted Hanson, "the biggest thing in his life was food."

A Foot, but Not Bigfoot

Unknown

NOVEMBER 30, 1990—Madison has once again left its tracks across the pages of the nation's supermarket tabloids. This time, it's Bigfoot.

In the November 27 edition of the *Sun* is a story headlined "Mystery of Bigfoot's Foot." The story quotes "Frank Lorenzo, a cryptozoologist from Oregon," who says he "had no doubt that the mysterious foot, found on a downtown street in Madison, Wisconsin, earlier this year, belongs to the legendary monster."

"The foot, which had no skin and had been severed below the heel, could belong only to Bigfoot, claims Lorenzo, who has examined it," the article said.

The *Sun* story quotes Lorenzo as saying he is "at a complete loss for an explanation as to how the foot came to be found in Madison." The story also quotes John Stanley, an assistant Dane County coroner, as saying the foot is definitely not human.

The *Sun*'s story apparently is a colossal exaggeration of a short news story from last January, which reported that a foot found in downtown Madison, in the 200 block of North Carroll Street, was from an animal. At the time, no one could tell what sort of animal the foot came from, but Stanley noted then that the foot was found outside a Madison Area Technical College classroom, where the skill of taxidermy was being taught. Stanley said he is pretty sure "a student from a taxidermy class dropped it on the sidewalk."

Stanley said Thursday he has never been contacted by the *Sun* newspaper. Further, it had since been determined that the foot was from a bear, and a small one at that.

"If it belonged to any 'foot' it would have to be Littlefoot, not Bigfoot, because it was so tiny," said Stanley, perhaps setting himself up for yet another tabloid quote confirming the existence of a Bigfoot family reunion in Madison last winter.

Stanley said a Madison pathologist and a Madison anthropologist have confirmed the foot belonged to a bear. The foot was also "X-rayed, viewed, and compared" and, for the last time, it came from a bear.

Also, said Stanley, there is no record of the person identified in the *Sun* story as Frank Lorenzo, "cryptozoologist," ever viewing the foot.

Violinist of the Night Shift

Bill Matheson, 1909–1993

MAY 17, 1993—Bill Matheson left a note with his daughter saying that when he died, she should send a copy of the obit to me in Madison.

He died May 5 in Duluth, Minnesota, and, judging by the nursing home mentioned in his obit, he had moved from his basement apartment. He was eighty-three. So, in the mail from Duluth came Matheson's obit.

Matheson wrote me a letter in 1989, out of the blue, wondering whatever happened to WHA radio hosts Cliff Roberts and Ken Ohst. (They had died.) It seems that Matheson, a concert violinist, worked the midnight to eight o'clock shift at the Duluth Water Department pumping station. Over the course of twenty-five years, he had tape recorded WHA radio programs, filling five hundred reels of seven-inch tape. He also cross-indexed the contents on thirty-eight thousand three-by-five cards. His prize, though, was his tape recordings of the fifty-album set of Franz Liszt keyboard music, broadcast on WHA on Sunday nights over two years, all by the great pianist Gunnar Johansen. (He died, too.)

After I had written a column about his tape-recording collection, one of his several daughters wrote me a kind letter detailing her father's love of music and his efforts to keep his daughters interested in music.

His obit says he "devoted his life to music through recordings, teaching, and rebuilding mechanized musical instruments. He was a solo violinist, and he enjoyed relationships with such well-known musicians as Victor Borge, Paul Badura-Skoda, and Gunnar Johansen. He assisted Liberace in a Duluth appearance in the early 1940s. In the 1930s he owned the Matheson School of Music and Dance in Grand Rapids. He also owned the American Conservatory of Violin and the Blue Note Cafe, both in Duluth."

But, and this is another reason I read the obits, Matheson did more than that: He was a president of the Duluth Chess Club. He was in the Civilian Conservation Corps, laying rocks and digging up bricks. He was an oiler on the SS *Jack*. He worked in the Chicago stockyards and served as "stationary engineer" in the US Treasury Building in Washington, DC. He worked for the water department for twenty-nine years, and he studied karate in 1986. He rebuilt a Weber Reproducing piano—an eight-foot grand piano—from top to bottom.

So that was Matheson: a violinist who could lay bricks, a father who loved music, a grandfather who learned karate, a night-shift engineer who loved to listen to Liszt on the radio, the guy in Duluth who worked with Liberace.

The Chimney Skeleton

Unknown

SEPTEMBER 12, 1993—Skinny. Real skinny. Small. But dead. Real dead. Bones and clothes dead.

The facts haven't changed since he was found in the chimney of a building shared by a music store and a sports card shop on University Avenue four years ago this week.

No one ever claimed him. The corpse was never associated with any known political causes. Angry letters are not written on his behalf, demanding justice. Once a year his story is repeated in this column. It is a curious enough story that maybe someone, somewhere, will remember something to solve this murder, to identify this lost soul.

Surely it was a murder? Perhaps you have heard of it. It is called the "Skeleton in the Chimney" case.

The chimney was 11.75 inches in diameter. At the bottom of that clay-lined chimney one Sunday morning in September 1989, the owner of the music store shined a flashlight into the cleanout, trying to trace a water leak.

He saw a skull.

Later, when all the bones had been removed from the chimney and examined, officials identified them as belonging to a young white male, about five feet five inches tall, with brown hair and a slight overbite. The man was probably twenty years old when

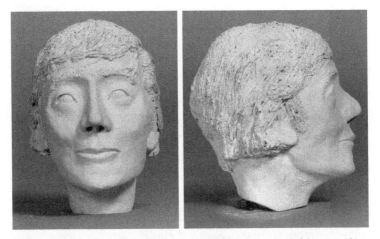

Experts at the Smithsonian Institution made this re-creation of the victim's facial structure based on the shape of the skull. MADISON POLICE DEPARTMENT

he died. The body and bones may have been in the chimney for two years.

Investigators, with homicide detective James Grann leading the way, determined that only a very slim body could have inched, or been stuffed, down that chimney. Once in, no one could have gotten out. The victim's pelvis was broken in two places.

A few days after the bones were found, police released further details, revealing that the man had been dressed in women's clothing. He was wearing a sleeveless paisley dress with a matching belt, a button-down Oxford shirt, and a White Stag brand shaggy-pile sweater. He wore low-heeled, pointed shoes and a pair of socks, and he carried another pair of socks. He wore no underwear, bra, or undershirt. Also found in the chimney were an Iron Cross medallion, a butter knife, and a pocket comb.

At first, it was thought the victim was simply a burglar who got stuck in a chimney. But the clothes, the twenty-seven-foot height of the chimney, the broken pelvis, as if from a beating, point to foul play.

Speculation over this case continued off and on for about a year. Perhaps, some detectives thought, the person had been killed in the parking lot behind the building, perhaps because of the way he was dressed.

Every year about this time, I call Jim Grann and we talk about the case. The conversations are not long.

Experts at the Smithsonian Institution used the skull to re-create the victim's face in 1990. The re-creation shows the victim with a narrow nose, bushy hair, and strong chin.

This year's chat was no different than the others. "We haven't had any leads all year," he said.

The case has already made it into a book, *Bones, a Forensic Detective's Casebook*, by Douglas H. Ubelaker. He writes about face reconstruction and uses a photo of the Smithsonian's plaster bust of the Madison victim.

The remains of the "chimney guy," as Grann calls him, have not been buried. Grann is keeping the remains until the state crime laboratory staff is up and running with new DNA testing facilities. The remains will be tested before they are put to rest, Grann said.

The DNA tests will join the dental charts as evidence that one day may be used to give the chimney guy a name and, maybe, his killer justice. After those tests, "it would be nice to finally give the guy a burial," Grann said.

The case will remain on his "silent case" list.

As of 2021, the case remained unsolved.

Pioneering Policewoman

Mary Ostrander, 1933–1994

SEPTEMBER 21, 1994—On January 9, 1967, Mary R. Ostrander, an officer with the Madison Police Department for nine years, wrote a note to the police chief. "I respectfully request permission to [take] the promotion examination for the position of detective," she wrote, ever so politely.

On January 10, her supervisor denied her request—not because she was not qualified, or was too young or too short or too old, but because women could not become detectives in the Madison Police Department.

Nor, though they made arrests, could they carry guns, or handcuffs, or go through training. They were paid less for doing the same work. Mary Ostrander, daughter of a Green Lake County judge and a college graduate (as required to work in the department), was not pleased.

She was not finished, either, and before she retired in 1983, she had taken on the status quo in the police department on several occasions, winning back pay for female officers, training, the right to carry weapons, equal wages, and, eventually, detective status on par with her male colleagues.

Ostrander, a red-haired woman who was the size of a fireplug and, at times, just as tough, died Sunday. She had been seriously ill since last winter, and a combination of diabetes and kidney failure led to her death at age sixty.

Ostrander joined the police department on April Fool's Day in 1958, when women were ranked Police Woman I and Police Woman II. They worked with families, women, and children, served as liaison with social agencies, and worked cases that these days are known as "sensitive crime." She was proud to be a cop and led state, national, and international associations of policewomen.

Ostrander liked working with kids the most, said her niece, Sue Kozubek. What she said about children in 1969, after more than ten years of dealing with Madison's youngest incorrigibles, was something she really believed: "Children learn from the attitude their parents have toward other people and authority. Parents will brag about cheating on their income tax and then expect their kids to be honest. They do one thing and tell them another. You can't bluff kids. Kids can see through things that adults can't. Actually, some kids grow up okay in spite of their parents. Some kids live in places I wouldn't let a dog live in, and others have too much.

"Parents have to keep track of their kids. You'd be amazed at how many times we call and the parents don't even know where their kids are or whom they're with. Sometimes, amazingly enough, parents can't even describe their kids to us when they're missing."

Ostrander would cluck at such things, but not loudly. Early in her career she noted that male officers dictated reports to secretaries, but female officers had to type their own reports. She fought against inequities like that, too.

The day she retired, in 1983, she told me about her first and final police cases. Her first was an assignment to track down the person who was scaring the heck out of a babysitter. Ostrander turned up the babysitter's brother, who was mad at his sister because he had to do the dishes that night.

Her last case remains open. It was the murder of Julie Speerschneider, who left the 602 Club on a foggy March night in 1979, intending to hitchhike east on Johnson Street. Her body was found two years later in the town of Dunn near the Yahara River.

Ostrander shared the assignment on that case, and it bothered her mightily that it hadn't been cracked.

It is a point of silent pride, though, that today's Madison Police Department has a female captain, a female lieutenant, four female sergeants, eleven female detectives and detective supervisors, one female special investigator, and seventy-five female officers.

Rare Defender of the Middle Ground

Ralph Hanson, 1928–1996

JANUARY 25, 1996—Ralph Hanson always seemed a little puzzled by it all. Then inevitably, when the smoke cleared, he seemed to be the only one who could figure it out.

There he would be, wearing a tan coat zipped up to his neck, a red baseball cap, looking like your best friend's grandpa at a junior high school football game. Only he would be carrying a bullhorn that he would fiddle with for a moment before saying something, presenting yet another, perhaps calculated, glimpse at his fallibility. Watching him, you could imagine him saying, "Now how do you turn this dang thing on?"

This, the students would think, is the campus police chief? Maybe that's why everyone just called him Ralph.

Ralph Hanson died this week of a heart attack at age sixty-seven. Most will remember him as the university police chief who calmly met demonstrators with a bullhorn during the tumultuous sixties and seventies. He would be standing on the steps of some campus building, surrounded by uniformed police officers, many in riot gear. And he would tell the assembled demonstrators that no, you can't come in here. Or he would wait them out. He would almost always let them speak (with their own bullhorn). Later, he might show up along the sidelines of another demonstration, wearing a fedora, sport coat, and raincoat. Demonstrators who might have spent the past twenty-four hours throwing rocks or organizing affinity groups would wander by and say, "Hiya, Ralph," as if they were greeting a friendly bus driver. If someone flashed him the peace sign, he would flash it back.

From 1965 to 1991, Hanson ran the UW Police and Security (P & S, as it was known then) from an office on the second floor of an old falling-down brick building at Orchard and Spring Streets. The detective office could have been the stage for the old *Barney Miller* show.

He quietly retired from his job a few years ago. It wasn't so much Ralph leaving the job as that the job seemed to leave him. More of the shots were being called from Bascom Hall. The university police force was modernizing, in no small way thanks to Ralph, who fought to get a new, more modern police headquarters, which came to be known as the House That Ralph Built. This replaced a converted three-story dilapidated brick

UW Police Chief Ralph Hanson, pictured in 1972. A. CRAIG BENSON, *WISCONSIN STATE JOURNAL*

building, known for its hidden stairways and closets and inaccessibility. But along with the new headquarters arrived the computer era, and campus strife was no longer front-page news. Police work was changing.

Some of the younger police officers never knew the Ralph Hanson who, when he was a young state patrol officer in Maine, chased down two state prison escapees, first in his car, then on a horse, then on snowshoes. Finally, he captured them singlehandedly and returned them to prison. "The only time I ever drew my gun," he once said.

Modest to a fault, Ralph Hanson was protective of his campus and its residents and fiercely loyal to his men (and they were almost all men that he hired as cops, reasoning, one officer said years ago, that the best cop is a man with a wife, at least one kid, and a mortgage). He projected just the right image at just the right time in the history of the campus.

The thumb-suckers today call those days "turbulent," but those who were there usually use the words "chaos" and "an unholy mess."

On a single spring day in 1970, for example, the typical campus student would be facing much more than a simple residence hall choice between cheeseburgers, fries, and brownies for lunch. The teaching assistants might be blocking classrooms. And a student anti-war alliance would be planning an escape route from the southeast dormitories to the Lake Shore Path, with a stop at the Library Mall fountain to wash the pepper gas from their eyes. Legislators would be screaming for justice, businessmen would be pleading for protection, and aldermen with long sideburns would flout city hall decorum. And amid a protest of fifteen thousand strong and loud, not stopping for traffic lights would be normal. There was a war on, too.

At the time of the riots, the leaders of the two other police forces on Madison streets, the Dane County sheriff and the Madison police chief, were hard-nosed and hard-headed. Before the bombing of Sterling Hall, the university itself did not suffer much riot damage in comparison with the city, especially along State Street. Ralph Hanson and his officers never got the blanket reputation as head-bangers that those other two departments received, deservedly or not. They stood in the same line of fire, though.

Gary Moore, now working in the coroner's office but then a lieutenant in the campus police department, was with Ralph one riotous day when the chief was hit by a brick.

"That really got him mad, and he chased down the kid and grabbed him, and the kid hit Ralph a couple of times, and Ralph picked him up and threw him over a fence. When he found out the kid was seventeen years old, he just told him, 'You're too young to get involved with the police, you go home to your mom and dad.' The kid walked. He really was in tune to what the kids wanted or didn't want, he had a general knowledge of what kids were all about. He hated to see kids go to jail or get a record, and he honestly felt they had a right of free speech," said Moore.

Some of his officers—including Moore—occasionally thought he was too soft during the riots. "Of course, 'soft' then would be pretty harsh now," Moore said.

While his department was in the spotlight during more than a decade of riots in Madison, Hanson's strategy was to play it by ear. "He may have had a strategy, but we didn't know it," Moore said. "He would say, 'We'll see what they are going to do today,' and then we would react. We tried to have a plan, but it changed so much."

Ralph, who thought of his department as family, also had a soft touch with his officers. If his officers were honest, he could forgive most transgressions, and he had the power to do so. Hanson was not a university-educated law enforcement supervisor, but he knew the basics of running a family were forgiveness and flexibility. It was also the perfect demeanor for a fellow who had to deal daily with the delicate, inflated egos at the university. He hated to fire people. He hated it when people were dishonest with him.

Some Ralph Hanson stories are small treasures, perhaps apocryphal, but fitting the image of an avuncular police chief who was a lot more professionally adept than he let on.

He never carried a gun, for example, and it came to pass in the department that some of the younger officers doubted that he could shoot a gun. He never went to the range to practice, and the word was passed along to the chief that maybe he should take a few plunks at a target for the sake of appearance.

"So, Ralph borrows a gun from one of the officers, a four-inch standard thirty-eight special," remembered Moore. "He hadn't shot in ten years, but he had a grouping of less than ten inches on his target. He didn't bring it back, but someone else did, and it was posted in the court officer's office. Never again did anyone question if Ralph could shoot a gun. And when he heard that the target was posted, he took it down."

Most cops are nagged by crimes that go unsolved on their watch, and Hanson had one in particular that dogged him from 1968 until past his retirement in 1991. That was the murder of a student, Christine Rothschild, in May 1968. Her body was found outside Sterling Hall. The investigation uncovered no motive, no murder weapon, no witness, no suspect, and, even now, no solution. Like everything else that happened on campus while he was chief, that crime was personal to Hanson.

In a retirement interview, Hanson said he felt his job, a police officer's job, was to be neutral. He had to balance the constitutional rights of freedom of speech and assembly with the job of keeping the university open and preserving law and order.

Neutral. Now there's a word that isn't included in many job descriptions anymore.

Cat vs. Mole, Continued

Charlie, 1978–1996

MARCH 5, 1996—It was so warm a week ago Sunday I almost buried Charlie, our frozen pet cat. I couldn't get deep enough though, and the shovel kept getting mucked with clay, so I gave up after about two feet. Instead, I concentrated on using the shovel to whop the season's first mole.

The mole was boldly chugging along in broad daylight (how do they know?) next to the house foundation. This mole chose to push up a channel even as I was stumbling over the washed-out channels from last year.

The space two inches beneath my lawn has served as a mole gathering place for several years. All of the usual conventional methods of removal, except for traps, have met with little success. These included using a water hose to flood out the tunnels, smoke bombs, poison pellets, and insecticide to kill the grubs.

The unconventional methods were equally fruitless: Juicy Fruit gum in the tunnels, moth balls, even beer bottles set at an angle to catch the wind and make an irritating noise. All fruitless (unless you count the interesting sound made when a lawn mower runs over an empty Berghoff beer bottle).

Charlie's adventure with a mole is one of the fondest memories we have of our cat. It has to do with his amazing capture one afternoon of a mole and his indifference to it once it was caught.

Until that day, we assumed that moles were invincible. Charlie was lolling in the tall grass between mole-proofing beer bottles one afternoon when he suddenly showed the sort of quickness grown cats are loathe to exhibit publicly. Until that moment, we had assumed Charlie was incapable of catching anything but his breath.

Charlie the cat, pictured with Eivind Hesselberg. ELSE KARLSEN

The mole in question was a very brave or very stupid mole. Even the laziest cat will not put up with a small active furry rodent tunneling beneath his belly, and that is what this mole did. A mole outside its tunnel will take only a second to dig back into the earth, but this one had bothered Charlie enough so that with a swipe and a bite, the cat had the mole.

We watched as Charlie got the mole, gave it a swipe or two, dropped it, picked it up, dropped it, chased it for about a foot, then let it go. It was painful for me to watch as this mole escaped. Charlie retired to a pillow position, tail twitching.

This was several years ago. Charlie was never known for his critter-catching abilities, so this one stood out. Watson, a cat who died two years ago and who was in Charlie's class at the Humane Society shelter, was always bringing home his latest catch. Because the two were together so long, and because Watson is already buried in the back, it was decided that it would be a good place to plant Charlie, too.

We hadn't planned on Charlie not making it through the winter. I have heard of people who own old pets digging a hole in the fall in case Fido or Fluffy dies during the winter, but we didn't do that for Charlie. So, I came home from the Oregon Veterinary Clinic last month and wrapped up the cat's body, placed it in the freezer, and waited for the thaw.

Talking about this at dinner with the boys the other night, after watching *Milo and Otis*, a movie about a cat and a puppy, I reminded them that this was not Charlie, just his body. "He's in cat heaven, probably next to a wood stove, even if it's summer," I said.

"Yeah, he's probably not neutered, either," said Espen, no longer innocent.

While the family was gone that Sunday afternoon, it got warm enough to think about burying Charlie, and that's when I dug the hole. On the way back to the garage, I noticed the earth move in exactly the mole channel spot along the foundation I had tromped down earlier.

It was the mole, back again. I whopped it with the shovel, and all was quiet. The next morning, I noticed the earth was pushed up again.

Probably pallbearers.

Digging Up Graveside Traditions

George Bedessem, 1880–1967

MAY 5, 1996—I used to hear old George Bedessem talking to me while I mowed the grass and trimmed around the headstones at the Bangor Fairview Cemetery, the place where they bury Protestants in the town where I grew up.

George, who at the time was dead and was the only person buried in the cemetery I had known when he was alive, never said anything startling, usually "How are you doin' today?" or "You could use a haircut."

He never remembered my name when he was alive. He lived across the street from us, and I vacuumed his rugs for him for a quarter, sometimes fifty cents, on Saturday mornings.

So, it did not bother me that he never called me by name or that he was dead. His was the only voice I heard the summer I worked as a cemetery sexton. I shot gophers and mowed and trimmed and helped the village workers when a grave needed digging. The cemetery was on a hill overlooking the village, and the job helped me buy a Savage over-and-under shotgun for fifty-two dollars from Hussa Hardware at the end of the summer. What I kept from that summer were the shotgun, memories of George Bedessem, and an interest in cemeteries.

May, the month of Memorial Day, is a good month for cemetery stories. A recent caller to the paper wondered about which person is buried on the left, and on the right, when a husband and wife are buried next to each other.

The caller, a German immigrant, said his wife had died and, when he planned their tombstone, he realized she was to be placed on his left. In Germany, he said, she would have been on his right.

"As the monument is staked out, I will end up on the right," he told me. "All my life, out of respect, my wife has been on my right. But here, since when you got married the wife was on your left, she is on your left when buried. I am under the impression this might be one of those curious customs that came over with the Mayflower."

Fred Copa, at the Gunderson Funeral Home, knew the tradition: "It is a tradition because, as you are facing the altar when getting married, the wife is on the left-hand side, and when buried, she is there also." Changing the position, by request, would not be a problem, he said, but it is generally not a topic when arranging a funeral.

Gary Pechmann, at Pechmann Memorials, knew all about it, too. "In most cemeteries, the body is placed in the grave with the feet at the east and the head at the west, so the body in the grave is looking east to the rising sun," he said. "In some cemeteries, where all the markers are lined up and you read the marker facing east, the man is going to be on the right side and the woman is usually buried on the man's heart, or left side."

Catholic cemeteries usually place the man on the left and woman on the right, from the point of view of the person reading the marker, who would be facing west, he explained. Different cemeteries, especially Protestant ones, which have fewer restrictions to cemetery layout, may have different traditions, Pechmann said, but the most likely placement is husband on the right, wife on the left, facing east.

Generally, as you read a gravestone (or memorial, as they say in the business), you face west. But, as Pechmann noted, "the memorial can be at the head or foot of the graves, depending on each cemetery." This can be different even between sections of the same cemetery.

If this sounds all too complicated, consider the calculations that must be made by the gravestone company. Husband-wife graves along the same path, but on different sides of the path, would have inscriptions on opposite sides of the monuments, too. Double-depth graves are becoming more popular too, Pechmann said.

In the end, it doesn't make much difference to the dead person. Until someone unaffiliated with any religion actually comes back from the dead and says differently, though, a lot of people will go to their graves with the view in mind. In that case, the important direction isn't left or right, it's up or down.

Hats Off to Kindness

Willie Chatman, 1927–1996

JUNE 18, 1996—On cold days, Willie Chatman would move slowly in to the high-windowed pool area of the well-appointed Holiday Inn Select on East Washington Avenue. He would find a comfortable chair facing the sun, and he would stretch his old bones in the sunshine. He was a tiny man, and he did not take up much space.

One day last month, he died. Those old bones had cancer.

Chatman had been the shoeshine guy at the Holiday Inn for the past eight years. "Willie's Shoe Shine, $4 Shoes, $5 Boots," his sign proclaimed. If someone wanted a pair of shoes shined, Mr. Chatman was the one to go to. Not only the inn's customers, but men—and women, but mostly men—who wear good shoes from across the city would leave them at Mr. Chatman's to be cleaned and polished.

Andy Smith was one. Until this past week, he did not know Mr. Chatman had died. "I took some shoes in to be shined and Willie wasn't there. The front desk said he had passed away, and I was shocked," said Smith, who is in the banking business. "I know he had been trying to care for his aged mother in Milwaukee for a number of months, and he didn't have much money, no car that worked. There were a lot of people who really loved him."

"I thought it would be a terrible thing to die anonymously like that when so many people knew him," Smith said.

They knew him as customers, however, or as coworkers.

Mr. Chatman died at his apartment on Moorland Road. He had been ill at least since last winter, said Hollis Ashley, a soft-spoken man whom Mr. Chatman recruited to take over the Holiday Inn shoeshine business. Ashley remembers it was March 11 when Mr. Chatman asked him to meet him at the Holiday Inn to take over the stand. He agreed to become the new proprietor.

Ashley occasionally drove Mr. Chatman to the hospital or to medical appointments. "He said he was hurting so bad," said Ashley.

Several members of the Holiday Inn staff expressed sadness at Mr. Chatman's death. Most of them mentioned he was gentle, kind, helpful, quiet. Carla Reed at the front counter liked him. "He was kind of quiet. He didn't get paid much," she said. "He never seemed to have a bad word to say about anything. He drove a rundown car that broke down last winter. He loved his job. He would warm himself, sun himself in the pool area, early in the day, when the sun would really beat down in there."

Nannie Bernet works in the gift shop in the Holiday Inn, next to the shoeshine stand. "He was a beautiful person. He was my friend. I would bring him cake pieces and homemade bread. At the end he was shriveling. We were almost praying for him to go. He was in so much pain. Everyone liked Willie."

Ann Scarborough, a cousin in Milwaukee, said Mr. Chatman had lived in Madison for about ten years. Before that he lived in Milwaukee and shined shoes at a stand on Walnut Street. He also did odd jobs.

"His mother, Mattie Miller, and my mother are sisters," Scarborough said. He had a sister who, as they say, preceded him in death.

"He was a pretty nice guy," she said. "He had his problems, but we are all human, none of us perfect," she said, hinting at but not revealing any family secrets. None were pursued, either.

Mr. Chatman's cremation occurred two weeks ago at Wisconsin Memorial Park in Brookfield, arranged by a funeral home in Hales Corners. His ashes have been claimed by his friend Cynthia White. At this time, a memorial service is being considered, but no time or place has been selected.

Outliving the Obit

Thomas, unknown

MAY 25, 1997—After his death was reported in 1982, Thomas lived for a few years in a cabin with a dog. It wasn't until late in 1996, after becoming aware of the grave error, that he decided to call and ask for a retraction.

"I didn't even know I was dead," said Thomas, who asked to be identified only by his first name, in an interview last January.

Thomas had been reported dead on the newspaper obituary page in 1982. He was not aware of that notice at the time, and, if he had been dead, it wouldn't have mattered anyway.

Here is what that obituary said: "CHICAGO/MADISON— [Thomas], age 37, died Thursday, at the Veteran's Hospital in Chicago, Ill., of cancer. He was a former Green Beret Officer with the 7th Special Forces Airborne from 1962–1975, former prisoner of war. He leaves a 6-year-old daughter. He was one of the most decorated veterans of the Vietnam Conflict, a member of the VFW, the DAV, the Purple Heart Association, and the American Legion. He is buried in National Cemetery."

Thomas called the newspaper because a buddy he met at a reunion in Chicago "told me they had you for dead up in Wisconsin." When he heard that, he called around and at a local library he found a clipping of the obit. In a note to the newspaper, he supplied a copy of that obit, the name of his doctor, and a proposed "retraction" that said simply the first notice, printed fifteen years earlier, "was in error."

He left no return telephone number and only a post office box number for an address. It took a couple of weeks, a trip to Columbia County, and a few calls, but eventually I was able to leave a note attached to a door of a condo, asking him to call.

When he did, he told this soldier's story: Thomas is a Vietnam War veteran, Special Forces, with five tours to Vietnam, starting in 1964. He claimed to have retired at the rank of lieutenant colonel in 1977.

He said he did not know who called in his obituary in 1982, but he believes he was in the hospital in a coma at that time and wasn't doing very well. He said he did not have cancer but has had several other health issues. He had been shot in head, back, and hip. He suffered from seizures and has a plate in his head, he said.

"I don't know how or who put it in that I had passed away," he said. "I haven't been well for a long, long time."

Asked about the statement in his obituary about being much-decorated, he said, "I have a significant amount of awards I have never worn. I was simply surviving as best I could while helping others to survive, too. A lot of guys I loved very, very much were very, very dead."

Why did he continue to re-enlist, four times?

"I was tagged because I was a veteran with higher chances of survival. All I ever did was serve my nation, and after that, all I ever wanted to do was serve my friends," he said.

When asked how it would be possible to prove he is who he says he is, he provided his full name, his birth date, his parents' names and place of birth, his current residence out of state, and the names of his now-grown daughter, his American Legion Post, his favorite bar in Wisconsin, and his late wife. When he mentioned his wife, who did in fact die of cancer in 1982, he sounded very sad.

Since it was a mystery to him how his obit got in the newspaper, and he wanted to keep his privacy, he eventually decided not to ask the paper to print a retraction. He was slightly amused that anyone had noticed and remembered the apparently mistaken obituary.

As Memorial Day stories go, Thomas's is not an exciting one. It is a good sign, though, that one Vietnam vet who has gone through one or two hells in a previous life wanted to confirm that he is still kicking in this one.

Beyond First Impressions

Vivian Husting, 1911–1997

JUNE 22, 1997—Vivian Husting rode a city bus almost every day and, when she could, she would sit right behind the driver.

She never said a word, but every few minutes she would let out a sound, a "whew," and then settle back with her bags, her year-round stocking cap snug on her head and an itinerary as specific as any kept by better-smelling members of Madison society.

"It was a 'whew,' like she had seen something or was just making a comment," said Don Roeth, a Madison Metro driver who had Husting as a passenger for the past thirty-one years.

Husting volunteered at the Central Wisconsin Center for the Developmentally Disabled staff library on Monday and Tuesday mornings. She would type library cards. She would file and collate and package. She would avoid conversation but not because she was antisocial.

"She wouldn't say much, but frequently she would 'coo.' It sounded nice," said Lita Haddal, a librarian. "To her I was the rubber band lady. She always came to me for half of a box of rubber bands, never a full box."

Husting would take the G-Hilldale bus, getting on near Chadbourne Hall, almost every afternoon to eat a meal at the comfortable and well-appointed Hilldale Shopping Center, where she would visit the delicatessen at the Sentry Food Store.

"She would usually order two Johnsonville wieners, and they had to cost ninety-two cents," said deli worker Tara Renard. "If they didn't cost ninety-two cents, we would have to keep weighing two wieners until the cost came to ninety-two cents. Sometimes she would get a slice of ham. She would sit at the tables in the front, by Cafe Romeo, and eat. She was pleasant, she would sometimes complain. She always wore a stocking cap."

Husting, eighty-six, reputedly able to type one hundred words a minute, was found dead in her one-room apartment home on Friday, June 13, by police who were alerted because she had not shown up for her volunteer job. Fellow workers there called the Dane County Department of Human Services on Monday and Tuesday of that week, but the department did not notify police until Friday, after being contacted by Husting's brother-in-law, Hugh Moore.

Moore had been tracked down by the center library employees who were frustrated by Human Services' seeming indifference.

By the time police cut her screen window with a pocket knife and crawled into the stuffy one-room apartment at 29 North Hancock Street, Husting had been dead for about a week, probably of a heart attack. It was 5:55 p.m. The room was messy and cluttered, there was no food in the refrigerator, and the stove was on, the police and the coroner reported. She was identified by her Madison Metro bus pass.

The daughter of Gustav and Paula Husting, Mayville, she was buried in the Mayville Graceland Cemetery last Tuesday. A relative said she had lived in Madison since the 1930s.

Although she struggled with mental health issues for most of her life, Husting proved capable of caring for herself. Police records showed no contact between Husting and the Madison Police Department until they found her body June 13.

Moore said she never married and had done secretarial work at the university. Then, "her employment and her life's experiences caught up with her," he said, indicating, but not elaborating on, what began her mental illness.

"She started out at a county institution and was treated for mental problems and then released, and she more or less took care of herself. They put her into an apartment, and then she more or less volunteered her services to wherever they were needed. She was quite a typist and quite proficient in office work. At first, her relatives wanted to put her in a better apartment, but she wanted to make her own choices and have her own style."

Haddal said that based on her work at the library, she could tell that Husting was an intelligent woman. The center's records show she started in the volunteer program in 1983.

"She would coo and ramble and liked to talk about the movies she had seen and the things she went to see. She was pretty mobile, and she had her routes. I would see her at Hilldale. She had an apartment on the Capitol Square, and I would see her downtown, periodically at the Civic Center. I would see her there nicely dressed," Haddal said.

But her usual clothing choices included a stocking cap for all seasons, a heavy coat or sweater, brown stretch pants and jogging shoes, laces untied. She usually carried two bags. At the center, she would be given mittens and nicely knitted scarves and hats, but she kept to her preferences.

"In the summertime, her heavy clothes were probably a source of embarrassment to some people," said Moore, explaining that there could be an odor from her clothing and her bags.

Roeth, the bus driver, agreed. "Not everyone was happy to see her get on a bus because they didn't want her to sit next to them," he said. "Mostly she sat behind the driver. She liked me. She would get on the bus, and I would say 'Hi, Viv,' and she would look at me like, how did I know her name. No one would talk to her. One of the grandmothers [in the center's popular foster-grandparent program] told me she was a really sharp lady when she was younger."

Haddal was certain Husting volunteered her services at other places but was not sure where. "She kept busy, she had her bus routes, and she liked to cruise," said Haddal.

Moore, Husting's brother-in-law, said Husting had once volunteered, sorting clothing at a charity, but "they told her that they needed more than what she could provide, so she went to Central Colony" (the former name of the Central Wisconsin Center).

He also recalled how much she loved children. "She loved all the children she was related to and the children she never had. She was responsive to all the little relatives she had. She would send them dollar bills," he said.

Moore took her to the occasional medical appointment but only at her request. "No one could interfere in her life or tell her how to live. She simply would not tolerate that," he said.

When the people in the office where she worked called him, worried, he set out to find her. He went to Sentry, where employees also had noticed she had not been in for her two-wiener meals, and they were afraid something had happened to her.

He contacted Human Services, too, after he got no answer at Husting's door in the red brick, two-story apartment building on the corner of North Hancock and East Mifflin Streets.

"I rapped on the door and couldn't rouse her, I told them, and I said, 'I think she is dead.' The coroner asked if they should find out why she died, and I said no, she has had enough."

Susan Crowley, of the Dane County Department of Human Services, said the department could have better handled initial calls from Husting's worried coworkers. "I believe we did what we could to find out if we had any knowledge of the individual. That did take some time. I regret that occurred," Crowley said. "I have reviewed with staff to make sure that if the call appears to be life-threatening or of serious concern to the whereabouts, we immediately refer that caller to the police. It is not our primary job to check on people who have not been seen or [are] missing, but we want to be helpful."

"I have never known a personality that was like her," Moore said. "It took strength and courage for her to live. She was very good to everyone. She enjoyed taking a bus to different parts of the city, to East Towne Mall, where she would entertain herself by looking at the stores. She didn't have a telephone. That would have cost too much, and she wouldn't have been able to buy a bus ticket."

Moore said Husting might, at a glance, have been mistaken for "a typical bag lady," but that would have been a mistake, even if such a person existed. "She had a philosophy that was sometimes hard to understand, with all her problems," he said. "But she probably had a better insight into life, and the purpose of being on this planet, than anybody I know."

The Storytelling Cobbler

Michael J. Falci Jr., 1915–1997

SEPTEMBER 25, 1997—Michael J. Falci Jr., who sewed soles and leveled heels on State Street for more than forty years, died Tuesday at eighty-two.

As a fourth-generation shoe repairman, Falci operated Michael's Shoe Service at 545 State Street for twenty-seven years and with his father across the street for thirteen years before that.

Falci closed his business on State Street after the rent for his four-hundred-square-foot shop increased from about $200 a month to $1,175 a month. That was in 1983, and the landlord, Jerome Mullins, wanted to move Falci to an address off State Street and rent the space to a croissant shop and bakery. The current tenant is a cookie shop.

Falci's shop—really, Falci and his wife, Gladys, ran the shop—did not have a listed telephone number or a back door. His customers included students and governors and, during Camelot days, Jackie Kennedy.

When John Kennedy was in town campaigning one weekend, Jackie Kennedy broke a heel, Falci recalled in a newspaper interview. "I was asked to open on a Sunday so it could be fixed. Jack arrived in a taxi, and he played with the machines while I worked on Jackie's shoe."

Falci, a storyteller of some note, added that Kennedy never paid for the heel repair.

Michael J. Falci. DAVID SANDELL, *WISCONSIN STATE JOURNAL*

Falci did not retire after closing on State Street. Instead, he went to work part time at Cecil's Shoe Repair at Clocktower Court on Mineral Point Road.

"Up until two years ago, he would help out on odd jobs, come in one or two days a week so his old customers could see him," said Ron Burke, of Cecil's. "He did a lot of things extremely well that others could not do. Such as recovering ladies' heels, no one liked doing that kind of thing, but he would take the time to do it. He was crusty, but that was the nature of the time and place he grew up.

"Mike was very efficient, his craftsmanship was very good, and he did not waste time or resources, probably because he grew up in a time when there wasn't a lot to work with," he said.

Burke said Falci worked for the military during World War II repairing combat boots. "He would talk about that, about fixing boxes and boxes of combat boots. His customers came from far and wide to see him. They will be very sad that he is gone."

Madison's Fallen Angel

Angel Babcock Burns Richardson, 1921–1997

SEPTEMBER 28, 1997—Most people thought they knew who was sleeping in the stairwell. Most people knew the small lump in the matted coat was Angel, and most people did not care to know any more.

Poor them. Or as Angel could say in perfect French, *quel dommage*. There was, it appears, a lot to know.

Angel had what is generally known as a thought disorder. She saw snakes and conspiracies everywhere, and for decades she slept in the dirtiest store entrances, the loneliest stairwells, and the finest libraries in Madison. A homeless woman who suffered from kyphosis, a spine curvature that causes a hump on the back, she was so stoop-shouldered that she could not tolerate the pain of sleeping in a prone position.

Enough Madisonians and kindhearted police officers remembered Angel to donate more than one thousand dollars for her modest tombstone a couple of weeks ago. She died last June at the age of seventy-five.

Angel Babcock Burns Richardson was more and less than she seemed. Born into wealth in Madison, she spent periods of her youth in the capitals of Europe with private tutors. Her family received and sent mysterious, coded letters in French during World War II. Angel was once in line to inherit part of the proceeds from the sale of an entire city block in Chicago.

She gave birth to identical twin sons in 1944. Later she was sent to a mental institution. Surviving family members say Angel's husband took the twins to the West Coast in 1946, told them their mother was dead, and was never seen again.

What some might call her delusions, though both amusing and confusing to those who knew her only as a homeless old woman, were actually rooted in the realities of long ago.

Angel may have been in an institution until the early 1960s, when she worked for at least two years in the mailroom at the University of Wisconsin Extension building, a job her mother, Jessica Cady Burns, helped her get.

It was in the late 1960s and early 1970s that she became a fixture on the streets of downtown Madison, and it is from those days that most people remember her.

Downtown habitués would be surprised to realize Angel left her haunts in 1995, when a couple of officers hustled her off the streets and into University Hospital, then to Mendota Mental Health Institute. They tried to get her into a nursing home, but she wouldn't go.

It was Goodwill Industries that eventually found her a spot in one of their adult family homes in Sun Prairie in February 1996. There, with the help of medication, she was transformed. She loved to go out for dinner and smoke cigarettes. Unable or unwilling to lie down, she slept sitting in a chair.

After years on the streets, she spent the last eighteen months of her life eating ice cream and cream of asparagus soup and drinking tea.

On the streets, people had looked very quickly at, and then away from, Angel, for she was quite a sight. She squinted through blue eyes usually and mostly covered by a very bad wig, usually tied on with a scarf. She may have reached four feet tall, standing, though she was stooped in a permanent bent position. Though she spent many cold Wisconsin winters on Madison's streets, her warmest coat was cloth, a brown fuzzy one. Or she wrapped herself in a blanket or two and shuffled along from the City-County Building to State Street, to either Memorial Library, where her younger brother Jerry, a respected archivist, bridge player, stamp collector, and librarian who died in 1993, once had worked.

Angel ate breakfast at Memorial Union. Her movements were often dictated by where she could smoke cigarettes. She loved to smoke what she called "my delightful cigarettes." When she had a choice, they were Newports.

Police officers would say hello, just to make sure she was doing all right for the day.

"There were quite a few who looked out for her welfare and kind of kept an eye out for her, or watched for signs that she wasn't feeling well. We always made some contact to make sure she was okay," said Dale Burke, a lieutenant in the UW–Madison Police Department.

At the library, remembered Burke, Angel would find the study room that was open until the wee morning hours. This is where she would sleep. When she was moved out by security guards, she usually returned to the City-County Building.

Judy Tuttle, a former circulation librarian at Memorial, had her minor battles both with Angel and with the security guards on Angel's behalf. Angel had a borrowing card, which Tuttle had to revoke because she kept losing books. She still was allowed to enter the library, though, to read and to sleep. She would hide there, too, and try to stay overnight. She read mysteries and French literature in French.

Otherwise, she told her friend and protector, Dennis Reno, a Madison Police Department lieutenant who knew Angel for twenty years, that she spent a part of her days checking on her "parolees"—a mystery that might be related to what she did in Europe before World War II.

"I knew who she was, but I got to know her better about eight to ten years ago when I moved to the traffic [office]. She would come in when she was short of her Social Security money. I would loan her twenty dollars. She would come in at the first of the month and give me my twenty dollars back. I just kept the twenty dollars in my desk drawer and just recirculated it. She always paid me back."

Most of her money, said Reno, went to pay for taxicab fares to various restaurants, including Embers and the old Black Bear Lounge. "She would leave a big tip so she could stay there for hours. She got kicked out of a lot of places, though," Reno said. "She was bullheaded and wouldn't take help from anyone."

Angel Richardson.
RICH RYGH, *CAPITAL TIMES*

Reno said Angel's late brother, Jerry, who was a historical librarian at the Credit Union National Association, every month would deposit a couple of hundred dollars into an account at First Wisconsin, which Angel could withdraw when she needed it. At one time, the Social Security Administration found out about the brother's support and threatened to reduce Angel's meager monthly check by the amount of the support, Reno said.

Jerry and Angel had a falling out long ago, his friends said, and though he tried many ways to help her or set her up in an apartment, in the end all he could do was deposit the money in the bank.

Angel refused welfare or help from the county social workers, Reno said. Perhaps her background had something to do with her stance. "She used to say she was related to the Queen of England and that her family had billions of dollars," Reno said.

Kathy Mason, of Lake Oswega, Oregon, married one of Angel's twin sons, Paget Daniels Richardson, in 1964. (The other son was named Graham Henry Richardson.) They had a daughter, Cinthia Calkins, now thirty-three, who is Angel's granddaughter. From interviews with Mason; Calkins; Madison attorney David Uphoff, who represented Angel's brother; Bob Davis, a friend and co-worker of Jerry's; and information from historical records comes this description of Angel's background:

Angel's mother, Jessica Cady, was born in 1893 to an important Madison family, related to the Fullers, scions of the city's industrial and arts worlds and long associated with Maple Bluff. She married Raymond Babcock, and they had two children: Angel in 1921 and Jerry, born in New York, in 1922.

In Jessica's belongings, inherited by Calkins, were old photographs of the young family taken in various European capitals. That would have been before Jessica divorced Babcock and married Jeremiah George Angus Burns in 1932.

It was clear that Angel's childhood was a European adventure. A key is contained in a short biographical sketch included in *A History of Wisconsin Credit Unions* written by Jerry Burns: He and Angel moved to Italy for a year when they were very young. They then lived in France for several years and, in 1934, moved to England, returning to Madison in 1936.

Their years in Italy and France might have been made possible by Jessica Burns's relatives: She was a cousin of Jessica Haskell Fuller, a famous soprano who is buried in Madison's Forest Hill Cemetery. (Madison history buffs may recall the Fuller Opera House.)

Angel's father, Raymond Babcock, might have been an architect, but there is scant record of his existence. It is also a mystery to remaining relatives what Jeremiah Burns, Angel's stepfather, did for a living. When the family lived on East Gorham Street in the 1940s, her stepfather's occupation was listed as simply "USA," meaning he worked for the government. He later worked for the old state Department of Transportation, according to city directories of the time.

Angel's mother, described as outgoing, was an office worker and also clerked in a stylish Madison dress shop, Leah's Smart Shop, on State Street, according to acquaintances and city directories.

Mason said that among the items her family inherited were many old letters, written in French, in what appears to be a code. That, and the fact that Angel, Jerry, and their mother were very secretive about their past, might have led to the rumors of the family working for the French Underground during and before World War II.

"When Jerry died, we went through their things," Mason said. "He had left his mother's room intact for fifteen years, almost as a shrine. In the drawers were letters dating back to the thirties and twenties from Europe. They would go abroad with these relatives and stay with them. They traveled and bought jewelry and expensive, unusual items. We have some of them. There was some connection with the Ringling Brothers, I think, because we [inherited] some of their china," Mason said.

Angel married a man named Henry Richardson, "a sailor," Mason said. They had twin sons, red-haired like their mother.

"Two years after the twin sons were born, in 1944, she went into a mental hospital," she said. No one knows what caused her mental collapse.

Exactly where Angel went is in question, since her family was forever silent on the issue and confidentiality rules keep those records closed. A clue is contained in a letter sent to Goodwill Industries with a donation for Angel's gravestone. The writer, a woman who worked at the old Dane County Hospital in Verona, said she knew Angel when Angel was a patient there.

"The boys' daddy told them she was dead, and he brought them to Portland and put them in an orphanage. He remarried several times, and the boys were in and out of the orphanage," Mason said.

"It wasn't until we had been married for a number of years before he heard from Jessica, Angel's mother. She wrote and enclosed a letter from Angel. Until then, he thought his mother was dead. We were all just shocked," Mason said.

The Richardson brothers' story has its own bizarre twist. The twins entered the Navy and were assigned to submarines based in San Diego, she said.

"They used to switch identities, and that got them into trouble with the Navy," said Mason, who was married to Richardson for seven years.

She knows that one of the two twins is dead, but because of the brothers' history of identity switches, she doesn't know which one.

Their daughter, Cinthia Calkins, however, is the last link of the family chain. Jessica Cady Burns—Angel's mother and Cinthia's great-grandmother—kept in contact with Mason in Oregon. So did Jerry Burns. After Jerry's death in 1993, police helped Mason meet Angel in Madison. Mason said Angel did not believe she had a granddaughter.

Calkins now has the remnants of the family's history—photographs, letters, china, steamer trunk, and all—in storage in the state of Oregon.

Mason and Madison attorney David Uphoff also were able to shed light on Angel's frequent ramblings about her financial status. She was rich, or was going to be rich, she often said, possibly referring to an old family trust, the Caroline E. Haskell Trust, which Uphoff said traces back to the ownership of an entire city block in Chicago.

That trust might have been worth millions, and Angel may have thought she was going to inherit it, but in fact the family annually received only "a very small, fractional interest, divided multiple times." At most, Angel's mother might have received a couple of hundred dollars from the trust, an asset she assigned to Cinthia.

But that trust, said Mason, is a ninety-nine-year trust and soon will be dissolved. She has been told by attorneys for the Northern Trust Company in Chicago that its value of five million to seven million dollars will be shared among fewer than one hundred descendants, her daughter Cinthia among them.

Angel's last months were spent in comfort. Mary Grabot, a housing specialist for Goodwill, recalls picking up Angel from Mendota. She had no belongings. "She always said she wanted to go home. We told her she was going to a new home, and we expected some reluctance, but she accepted it," said Grabot.

Steve Anacker, who with his wife, Bonnie, lived in the adult family home where Angel and at least two others stayed, described her as "very gracious, very courteous, a good chatter." She loved to go out to eat, he said, describing her manners as "elegant."

Angel, who learned her manners in France and Italy, practiced them to the end, Anacker said. Her favorite spot to eat in Sun Prairie was in the smoking section of Sir Hobo's, a family restaurant.

She was buried in one of the oldest sections of Forest Hills Cemetery in a plot her family has owned since 1914. There rest the Fullers, the Hobbins, the Haskells, the Cadys, and one Angel.

More than an Organ Donor

Patti A. Heim, 1956–1997

JANUARY 25, 1998—On the afternoon of November 22, an eighty-seven-year-old man in Shelby, North Carolina, lost control of his pickup truck on Highway 74, starting an accident that would eventually take the life of Madison native Patti A. Heim, known to one and all as "Pete."

Pete Heim was forty-one, a University of Minnesota journalism graduate, a friend of stray animals, and a totally blameless victim of a traffic accident. Her unusual nickname derived from Pickle Pete, mascot of a popular Madison drive-in restaurant.

"She was the kind of person who would give you the shirt off her back, and I should know because I sometimes got the shirt," said Susan Underwood, Patti Heim's sister, younger by a year.

So, faced with the ultimate of decisions, Susan and Patti's mother, Jinny Heim, knew what the dying Pete would have wanted.

"I feel she was guiding me," said Jinny, of the decision on November 30, the day her daughter was allowed to die, to donate as many of Pete's organs as possible: her heart, her kidneys, her liver, even her thigh bones, and whatever else was needed.

Most organ-donation stories are centered on the recipient, the Heims have realized, so they wanted some small notice made of their daughter, the donor. Last Wednesday morning the Heims recounted the accident, their response, the eight days Pete was on life support in the Carolina Medical Center, and the donation permission.

Pete was one of four children—including three daughters—of Jinny and Bob Heim, a Madison family. When the decision was made to donate her organs, said Jinny, "My only request [to the donation coordinator] was that I told him I would not allow him to put my daughter in a corner and keep her there while they wait to do this."

They didn't. The process went quickly. Once the decision was made, at 10:30 a.m. on a Sunday, Pete was officially pronounced dead at 4 p.m. "We have nothing but praise for that trauma unit," Jinny said.

The paperwork was the only sore point, but that might have been because the family was under stress and the person in charge was, said Bob, "cold-blooded" and bureaucratic.

Of course, the organ donation did not end Pete's story. Her belongings were donated, and notes of condolence came in from all across the country.

The Heims, however, had unanswered questions, mostly about the people who received their daughter's organs.

Debbie Gibbs, of LifeShare of the Carolinas, a nonprofit agency that arranges transplants, locating donors and recipients, said donor families are naturally curious, but the agency will not identify the recipients except in general terms. The Heims know now, for example, that a forty-six-year-old father of two young children received Pete's heart.

Gibbs acknowledged that news about transplants focuses more on the recipients because "usually the recipient is so happy and is telling everybody, and the [donors' families] are not always so willing to tell their stories. Sometimes they would rather keep it private."

Likewise, said Gibbs, recipients are not told the identity of the donor, except in general terms. The recipient may feel some guilt, for example, and it is possible that, if they met, the donor family and recipient would not get along, she noted.

Still, the Heims wish it were possible to make that connection. "I think people should understand that there is a lot of sorrow that goes with this," Bob said.

And, said Jinny, "Perhaps in time they may want to know more about her."

The couple do not believe that their daughter lives on in someone else's body, but they want the recipients—if they one day wonder—to have the opportunity to know more about Pete.

For now, Jinny and Bob can write a general letter describing Pete that LifeShare may share with the organ recipients. Perhaps the forty-six-year-old father of two, who has Pete's heart, will never know more personal details, such as that she was a "vibrant, giving, healthy girl" who had a button that said, "I Survived Catholic Schools," and a "Patti wagon" she took to the farmers' market, and who had planned to move back to Minneapolis October 1 but was delayed.

And the recipient will not know that Pete's father, a crusty ex-marine who worked for forty-one years for A.J. Sweet, when asked how the donation process could be done differently, could only blink and say, "It would be better if you just never had to go through it."

And the recipients would not know that when a nurse suggested Pete's feet might be cold in the hospital, Jinny brought a pair of socks for her. Jinny still has those Pete-scented socks. "I keep them in my drawer," she said softly.

And the organ recipient who lives because Pete Heim died will not know that when it came time for Pete's heart to be saved, a trauma nurse named Linda witnessed the last time Jinny was allowed to hold her daughter and say, "I love you. We will remember you."

Perhaps the Heims can divine some comfort from something that happened at the hospital when Pete died.

At the trauma unit in the Charlotte hospital, all of the patients' families wait in one area and are allowed to visit for only fifteen minutes, four times daily. When those fifteen minutes show up, a virtual cattle call of relatives surges to see their loved ones, most of whom are in bad shape. With little privacy in the ward and the sharing of the waiting, the families get to know one another quite well.

On the day Pete died, a woman who had shared the Heims' tragedy with her own for several days went up to Bob and gave him a big, long hug.

"Thank you," he said, "but I don't even know your name."

"It doesn't matter," she said.

The Cat That Came Back

Rover, Unknown–2000

FEBRUARY 6, 2000—Rover, an eccentric gray cat with a raccoon-like walk, is dead—again. This time it should take.

Rover's first grave was dug in September 1992, beneath an apple tree in the backyard of the Westmorland neighborhood home of UW–Madison assistant professor Diana Mutz.

Mutz had just moved here, and Rover, a gifted cat in the sense that someone found him and gave him to Mutz, found a hole in the fence and wandered away. Mutz was sure Rover wouldn't get very far, but she was worried because the cat collar he was wearing had her New York telephone numbers on it.

Sure enough, when she called her old office the next day, she was told the Humane Society in Madison had called that morning and reported a cat named Rover with a red collar had been hit by a car and killed. The Humane Society confirmed the news.

"I came home from work, and I was moping about, kicking myself about the hole in the fence," Mutz said in 1992.

She decided it would make her feel better if Rover was given a proper burial, so she dug the grave and enlisted a friend to go along and pick up the dead cat. At the shelter, she was given Rover's red collar. "Then the guy brought out the cardboard box with the body in it and said, 'Here's the gray cat with the white paws,' and I said my cat did not have white paws."

Her friend looked in the box. It contained a dead cat, but not a dead Rover. Rover—who was, in fact, alive—was instead in the back room in a corner cage, probably telling all the other cats that he had been framed.

Rover had not been hit by a car. Instead, a neighbor reported him at-large, the animal control officer picked him up, and some sort of mix-up with the collars ensued at the shelter. The Humane Society apologized, but Mutz was issued two tickets, one for allowing Rover his freedom and one for not getting a license. Rover plea-bargained to the at-large charge, and Mutz paid a twenty-five dollar fine. That was 1992.

Eight years passed. Now it is 2000.

Last week a card arrived from California, where Mutz and her math professor husband, Robin Pemantle, are on a nine-month sabbatical at Stanford University. With them are son Walden, four, and daughter Maria, two. Rover made the trip, as did another cat, Rory (a blotch of a cat, short for Rorschach), and a dog, Moxie.

The card announced the death of Rover, of cancer. He was in his teens, Mutz suspects, and the loss was especially traumatic for the children. The card described Rover as a rescued stray with a horrible sense of direction.

"He became widely loved by us for his doglike nature and uncharacteristic pacifism; he frequently shared a chair in the backyard with a chipmunk, and he never successfully hunted anything. Rover is remembered for his love of overeating, his short-term addiction to Valium, his raccoon-like walk. To our knowledge Rover has no offspring, though he attempted many times to produce half-kitten/half-blankets."

Rover was buried weeks ago in a backyard in Berkeley. That, however, is old mews.

Not surprisingly, Mutz said: "We had a strange thing happen."

A resident of their apartment building, knowing the Mutz

family had at least one cat, knocked on their door. "He had seen us carrying Rover's body.

"He said he had a cat in the basement garage inside the engine of his car and could we help get him out," Mutz said. "We found a total greaseball of a kitten in his engine. We took him to the vet, and he wasn't doing very well. Our kids immediately said Rover must have told the kitten that this was a good place."

That was a couple of weeks ago. The first week, the vet warned them the kitten might not make it. It would not eat anything. "Three days ago, I let him out to sort of interact with our other cat, and he marched right out to the screen porch and started eating the dry dog food. Now he's gaining weight, and all he eats is dry dog food."

In this life anyway, his name is Milo.

Footnotes on a Local Legend

Cecil Burke, 1926–2000

MARCH 28, 2000—One sunny day last year, a group of aging hipsters gathered in the backyard of a West Side home. They had not been together in one place in many years. Drinking beer, eating brats, comparing notes and family moves and additions, they reminisced as the minivans unloaded.

Into the backyard walked an ex-flower child, Ann, now in her late forties. She brought her daughter, Gina. A member of the assembled looked at the old friend's feet.

"Hey, are those Cecil's?" he asked.

"Yes," she said, "originals."

And her daughter was wearing a pair of Cecil's sandals, too.

"Cool," they said.

Ann bought her sandals in 1972 or 1973; Gina bought hers in 1996. "I've had them resoled, re-everything, many times," Ann said.

To own a pair of sandals from Cecil's Sandals in the 1960s and 1970s was to be—to be envied, to be copied, to be watched closely for other displays of coolness.

Cecil Burke, who died last week at the age of seventy-four, must have been aware that he was a Madison legend and his sandals were venerated cultural images. But he just kept on, in little shops, making sandals and some vests and fixing anything leather that was broken.

The buzz in marketing is branding. Companies spend lots of money figuring out how best to get their brand known to and trusted by the public.

Branding experts might want to start where Cecil did. He and the shop's workers over the years provided personal service and created a high-quality product at a reasonable price. And they could fix it. The same philosophy is followed by Cecil's son, Ron, at a shoe repair shop on Mineral Point Road.

Cecil Burke. CAROLYN PFLASTERER, *WISCONSIN STATE JOURNAL*

Even competitors liked Cecil. Sally Kopecky, who has run the Monroe Street Shoe Repair shop for twenty years, was taken in by Cecil as a sort of apprentice. He knew when he hired her that she had already bought shoe repair equipment and would probably one day open a competing shop.

Kopecky knew that she needed a mentor, someone who could teach her the details of shoe repair benchwork, and that's why she went to Cecil. He was a funny, patient mentor, Kopecky said last week after hearing of Cecil's death. He would stop by every few months to say hello or would be instantly available for consultation if there was a problem with shoe repair equipment.

There was a surprising lack of information about Cecil in the morgue of old clippings of the *Wisconsin State Journal* and *Capital Times*. There was only one old clip from each paper, the best a feature story in the *Times* from 1964 in which Cecil opened up and talked about his first sandal customer. A female student wanted him to make a pair of sandals, something he didn't want to do and didn't know how to do. At that time, he only repaired shoes; he didn't make them.

But she persisted, and he fashioned a pair. The sandals must have looked good because, he said, that first customer brought back ten more. A law student who had taken to using the back of Cecil's shoe repair shop as a quiet place to study helped Cecil figure out how to attach straps to the first sandals, and an art student contributed designs. Cecil said he enjoyed not only making the sandals but the selling and fitting of the sandals.

Every pair was custom made; that was the deal. It was a pretty good way to establish a brand, but it couldn't have been done without Cecil.

Memories of a Stonecutter

Oddvar Karlsen, 1916–2000

JUNE 18, 2000—It was the spring of 1976 and I was sick of trying to memorize the European edition of *Time* magazine.

My girlfriend, Else, told me her father, Oddvar Karlsen, always read *Time* magazine. I was meeting Else's parents for the first time and, eager to make a good impression, I had read the magazine forward and backward.

I took the train from Oslo to Eidanger, a village on the southern coast of Norway, a village where the train no longer stops.

During dinner, I casually started a conversation by slyly mentioning that I had "read in *Time* magazine this week . . ." Until then, Oddvar had barely said two words to me, but he suddenly perked up and started quoting *Time* and, for good measure, *Newsweek*, too.

He never told me what he thought of me marrying his daughter a couple of months later in the Oslo city hall. Nor did he pass judgment on my taking his daughter away from Norway, first to Asia and then to America.

When he died two weeks ago at the age of eighty-three, I looked back at the few times I had written about him. Once I described him as "an old man who has the biggest hands I have ever seen. He has little tufts of hair growing from his ears and his friendly, deep-set eyes water when he talks about his work."

That was a column about the lost art of stone cutting. I wrote that although he had been retired from stone cutting for several years, he still got calls from people in his business asking him to come out of retirement to do little jobs they could not do. After selling his one-man shop, he remained in demand because his ancient skills were needed by the new stone-cutting businesses.

Say, for example, an old handsome tombstone—in the trade, they're called monuments—with a certain script needed to be updated. To keep the script uniform, the services of an old master were needed. The new stone-cutting methods were fine, but they could not always duplicate everything from the old.

When he took vacations, Oddvar would always drive through cemeteries, looking at and taking photographs of tombstones, noting the color and grain and sparkle of different types, inquiring about the stone's origins just to test his own knowledge. He knew the stone from quarry to cemetery, from hillside to bank balustrade. The one time he visited Madison, he walked into the Capitol building, placed his big hands on the walls, the marble and granite columns,

Oddvar Karlsen, pictured with his wife, Gerd. ELSE KARLSEN

and said under his breath, "Beautiful stone." Much of that granite came from Norway.

I also wrote about Oddvar in 1994, when I spent a few months in Norway covering the Winter Olympics. Else had taken a one-year leave of absence from her job here to work back in her hometown in 1993–94, and our sons, Espen and Eivind, ages nine and six at the time, went with her.

I wrote that I was glad to have had the chance to be in my wife's childhood home for a couple of important moments in our sons' lives. One of those moments came on a sunny evening in May, sitting in the backyard at the picnic table, trying with the boys to carve a whistle by referring to a diagram in a book.

In the doorway that evening stood Oddvar—*mor-far*, which means "mother's father"—watching. He approached the table slowly and surveyed our mess. Wood shavings littered the ground, and failed whistles, carved to exact specifications of the helpful book, were starting to stack up.

Mumbling something that sounded like "that'll never work," he walked away and came back with a branch as slender as my little finger. As Espen, Eivind, and I watched, he quickly selected a short, straight section, tapered one end, notched it in the middle, and then cut a narrow ring at the other end.

He made a series of cuts into the ring that separated the length. Then he took the knife blade in between his fingers and started severely tapping all around the whistle to loosen the bark.

After several minutes of tapping, he twisted the length, and the bark loosened and was pulled off in one piece. He then cut a minuscule sliver of wood from the top of the tapered end of the barkless piece to the notch. Then he carefully slipped the bark back on and handed it to Eivind, who hooted away to his heart's content.

And then we were all little boys again, and we made whistles, lots of whistles.

In Search of the Simple Life

Simon Sparrow, 1914–2000

SEPTEMBER 28, 2000—Simon Sparrow, a "wise and just man" whose glitter in art and simple reverence in life made him an important national figure in folk art and a beloved local character, died Tuesday in a Madison nursing home.

He was eighty-five, and though he was heralded by art experts as, technically, an "outsider" or "naive" artist, his philosophy on life was anything but: "Life just is, and nothin' takes its place," he once said.

Sparrow started out selling his oil pastel paintings of devils and saints on campus for ten dollars. In 1989, one of his creations—and the amazingly detailed, intuitive collections of glass, beads, marbles, shells, garage sale scrap, and tin pieces were indeed universes within universes—sold for ten thousand dollars at auction.

His works have been shown at galleries and museums across the country, but most Madisonians might remember the slight, gray-bearded man as a blue-robed street preacher, with a pulpit as big as the State Street mall, with the Memorial Union as his sacristy and studio.

"To me, his art and personality and preaching all went together, it was just him," said Sparrow's son, Gabriel. Gabriel and his sister would tag along to watch his father draw at the Union. "He

Simon Sparrow. SCOTT SEID, *WISCONSIN STATE JOURNAL*

would pretty much sit there at the Union and draw, and people would flock around him and watch him draw for hours."

His main gallery outlet was the Carl Hammer Gallery of Chicago, which continues to showcase Sparrow's works, his son said.

Patrons of the old Henry's Restaurant on University Avenue might have discovered him first, though. A patron found Sparrow and his work in the cafe's parking lot in 1983, the story goes, and made it a mission to get him noticed.

Sparrow was unaffected by the acclaim that followed. He always insisted his true life's work was preaching, and he was equally consistent in crediting "the Spirit" for his art work.

His friends, he once said, would describe him as "wise and just."

The best thing about Madison, he once said, was that "nobody bothers me."

The worst? "Nothin' yet."

Explaining how he places various objects in his work, he said in a 1993 interview, "The Spirit just leads my hand to it."

Till Death Did They Part

Vade Henderson, 1914–2000
Russell Henderson, 1915–2000

DECEMBER 10, 2000—Vade Burkhardt, the daughter of a Viroqua carpenter, was in her thirties when she met Russell Henderson.

Russ had been married once already when he met Vade in Madison in the 1940s. He worked at Northwest Airlines, and she at the State Medical Society. Russ and Vade celebrated their golden wedding anniversary in 1997. They were as inseparable as a couple could be.

In their eighties, they moved to an apartment at the Meriter Retirement Center in July of 1998.

"They were happy here," said Kathy Groth, Meriter's housing director. "He really doted on her and cared for her. He was a total role model of a husband, so devoted and dedicated."

At times, the two seemed to have melded into one. "It was kind of cute. They even sort of dressed alike. They liked to wear browns and golds. They could be identified by the same color of their outfits," Groth said. "They were very affectionate, holding hands. He was this proper kind of guy, and she always looked at him so adoringly. When I visited, she would say under her breath, 'That Russ, he is just the best.'"

Their health started to decline noticeably in February of this year. "Russ was the strong one. He had prostate cancer, and it went to his bones. He got weaker and weaker, and then Vade started deteriorating," said Groth.

Vade became so weak she was moved from the apartment in the retirement center to a room in Meriter's adjoining nursing home. Russ stayed in the apartment, but he visited Vade several times a day. He took her for rolls in the wheelchair through the hallways. They went back to the apartment to spend time together.

"He would eat with her, feed her. He wanted to make sure she got nourishment," Groth said. "He wanted to completely be in her presence, and she wanted him to be there."

They knew they were dying. Russ did not want to die first.

"He wanted to make sure he lived longer than Vade so he could take care of her," said John Thomas, their longtime friend and pastor at Christ Presbyterian.

That was why Russ had what is called a "full code" order, directing that all means necessary should be taken to resuscitate him. Vade had a "do not resuscitate" order. "I think Russ was holding on to take care of Vade," Thomas said. "Neither one of them wanted to die without the other."

Russ was no longer being treated for the cancer that had spread to his spine. He was being treated for the pain.

"We were amazed at how he kept hanging in there, so motivated to being with her, even at the very end, when she came to see him," Groth said.

The very end.

Until Russ went to the hospital and was in intensive care, Vade was not aware how sick, how close to dying, he was.

"Last Thursday, Vade seemed to realize that Russ might not live very long," recalled Thomas. "It was the first time she seemed to be accepting of the fact that he wasn't going to make it."

Last Friday afternoon, a social worker took Vade to see Russ. "She told Russ that they would both be with Jesus, that he didn't have to struggle anymore," Thomas said.

She told him, "I will see you in heaven," according to Groth.

Vade returned to the nursing home, and Saturday morning she died.

Soon after, Russ was told his dear Vade was gone. And only then did he die.

Rolling through Life

Jeff Jodar, 1953–2001

MARCH 22, 2001—One of the first things Jeff Jodar said, when asked how he got around Madison from his starting point of an inoperable van in Lot 60 at University Hospital, was: "You would be surprised at where I can go in this chair."

Notice he did not say: "You would be surprised at where I can NOT go in this chair."

That was in 1996. It was just before the start of a Wisconsin winter, and Jodar was not looking forward to it. He was broke, he was out of food, he was living in a van in a hospital parking lot, he needed some medical attention, and he was not about to complain about any of that.

The fact that he did not have legs just made it easier for him to maneuver when he was beneath his van, a wrench in hand, a mechanic-related insult on his lips. Diabetes had claimed his legs, and his eyes were failing, too. He wore out two pairs of cycling gloves per summer month, four per winter month, pushing his wheelchair wheels.

He was a pretty good mechanic, which helped keep the van going for a while, and which gave him something to do between medical appointments.

Jodar, a former truck driver, had a kidney transplant at the University Hospital in 1987. Then he had a quadruple bypass.

In 1993, he lost his left leg to diabetes. Then, his right leg. It got to the point that it was easier for him, mentally and physically, to just park his van in a corner of the vast Lot 60 and stay there. Once, to get his mail, he rolled his wheelchair from Lot 60 to Milwaukee Street and back. It took twelve hours.

Fiercely and aggravatingly independent, he hated to be mistaken for a homeless person. His van had a cot and a sink and a stove and a television set. He used the bathrooms at the Lot 60 parking office. Jodar was not a problem.

In October 1996, the brakes failed on his van, he needed a new wheelchair, and his disability checks were short a couple of months. One day, talking about his considerable health problems, he allowed that those problems "don't really bother me very much." The problem was money.

A newspaper column in November 1996 resulted in several hundred dollars in donations to Jodar. A group volunteered to recondition his wheelchair, he got the brakes fixed, later he got a new used van (which he later crashed). His friend Mike Flood said Jodar cried when he read the many letters urging him to keep his spirits up and congratulating him for his ability to survive. He wrote thank-you letters.

Not much was heard from Jodar after that, though he continued to live in a van in the parking lot. He was not the sort of person who would make waves or get into trouble. He came close to death several times. When his health started failing two years ago, his friends got him an apartment in a hospice, but once he felt well enough, he left. He did not like being away from his van. His family chipped in to buy an RV, but in the end, he sold it and returned the money.

According to Stacy Meuer, who works at the University Hospital and whose husband, Greg Papendieck, grew up with Jodar, it became clear that Jodar needed an apartment, and he found a place at the DeForest Senior Apartments with the help of the Community Living Alliance.

"He didn't think he would like it, but they were so good to him there," Meuer said. "He had a nice little old lady on each side of him, and they sort of mothered him. He was real happy," said Meuer.

A couple of weeks ago, his health began to deteriorate. He still had a truck to work on and didn't complain, but a neighbor alerted the hospital. Jodar became weaker and weaker, had a heart attack, rallied, weakened, and was allowed to die. He was forty-seven.

"He was such an individual soul," Meuer said. "He was changing the transmission in his truck. He had to have his wheels."

Traveling Yesterday's Back Roads

Gary Hesselberg, 1945–2001

MAY 3, 2001 — One of the great things about being grown up is the chance to get in the car and just drive, take the roads you haven't taken in a long time, and stop where you haven't stopped before.

Last Wednesday, I drove to Bangor for my cousin Gary Hesselberg's funeral. He was his children's hero, one fine baseball player, and the inventor of a pretty good turkey call, "Ol' Hess." We even saw a turkey come out of the swamp of Fish Creek during the service in the Rockland Cemetery. We figured it was a scout sent by the turkey authorities to make sure this wasn't another one of Gary's hunting tricks.

After the funeral, back at my folks' place, my dad was showing a couple of his brothers a bundle of letters written by my grandpa, their father, while he was in France during World War I. I left them at the kitchen table, deciphering the old-timey handwriting of a kid a long way from the farm, wondering what chores he was missing, assuring his mother everything over there was "fine and dandy." He mentioned a fine sweater that a girl named Ragna made and gave him in Rockford before he left. That would have been my grandma.

I drove the back roads back to Madison, just for a chance to honk my respect as I drove by the old farm where Gary grew up on the way to Fish Creek Ridge. It was in these coulees that we learned to hunt. This was where my buddies and I parked our brothers' Chevrolets and drank warm Blatz, where we made out like fools with our girlfriends and learned too late what a hickey was. It was where we got the cars stuck, or planned holy revenge on guys from Sparta and Cashton, or skinned squirrels or shined deer. We always honked when we drove by the farm. We all knew Gary, and his brothers Al and Billy Junior, and his sister Cathy.

So, I honked again and headed up to the ridge past the Fish Creek Ridge Norwegian Lutheran Church and cemetery, and over to Highway 27, poking along behind an old pickup truck loaded with plywood. On to Highway 14 through Westby and Viroqua, where I slowed down to watch an Amish crew work on a house, and then Readstown, where I bought some grapefruit juice and peanuts and damaged goods coffee at the liquidator store.

I guess it was just my day to honk. I honked the car horn at road kill and at interesting trees and road signs, Farmall tractors, and old standby landmarks or buildings that used to be one-room schools or two-vat creameries. I honked when I went by my friend Richard Shackelford's place outside of Mount Vernon, where I once ate roasted goat.

It's funny what you remember about people who have died. I remember Gary on a tractor or wearing a baseball uniform and hitting the cutoff man. I had a friend named Wendy who died in a mountain climbing accident in Norway in 1975. Whenever I think of her, I see her reading a *Playboy* magazine, because she borrowed mine. My neighbor Bob Purcell died last Saturday. I remember him in yellow, because I always talked with him in the workshop on his Fitchburg farm where he repaired chain saws and sharpened chains. The shop was stacked with yellow greasy McCulloch chain saws. Bob was one of the good ones. Virginia Kidd was another. She died Sunday and had retired years ago, but I cannot picture her without a grandchild toddling along behind her.

The great philosopher Bruce Springsteen had a song called "Glory Days," about the best moments of life that pass you by, that are gone in the wink of an eye.

No, those moments aren't gone until you are.

Radio Villain

Tony Parrish, 1917–2001

AUGUST 16, 2001—Tony Parrish, eighty-three, a Madison native who pretended to die, loudly and often, when he played villains on popular radio dramas broadcast to the nation from Chicago in the 1940s, died Tuesday at a nursing home in Fort Myers, Florida.

Born Anthony Paratore to a well-known Italian family from Madison's Greenbush neighborhood, Parrish and his wife, Roma, ran the Villa Night Club, at 2302 South Park Street, in the 1950s and 1960s. He also ran TP's Liquor Mart, at 2430 Park Street, into the 1970s. His brother, the late Vito Paratore, operated a Park Street restaurant, Gen and Vito's Snack Shack, with his wife, Gen.

Parrish—a name he adopted when he started singing professionally—went from reading the farm news on Madison radio to an announcing career in New York City and Washington, DC, before heading to Chicago to work as a freelance actor, announcer, and nightclub singer.

A 1962 Madison newspaper article noted Parrish in the 1940s was heard regularly on *Today's Children*, *The Tom Mix (Ralston Straight Shooters) Show*, *Terry and the Pirates*, and *Jack Armstrong, the All American Boy*.

Joe Cerniglia, unofficial historian for the Greenbush neighborhood and its families, was a buddy of Parrish. "He was on all those radio serials out of Chicago, when Chicago was the national headquarters for radio shows," recalled Cerniglia. "He almost always played the villain. And the villain usually got killed in the last episode. One year he got killed thirteen times. On the Tom Mix program, he once played the villain Cesar Ciani. When his character was killed, he was so popular they had to resurrect the character the next season."

Parrish was in and out of the news in the 1960s and 1970s, once in a "hat box" case, where he was charged and acquitted of failing to report and pay taxes on $24,000 cash. He claimed that $14,200 of the amount was money found in a hat box, which had been left in a closet by his late mother-in-law. The other $10,000 came from cash he used to pay entertainers at his nightclub.

Cerniglia noted Parrish suffered from the same eye disease as his brother Vito and their father. All three went slowly blind due to a disease of the retina. Though blind, "he would always say when he met someone, 'You're looking good,' " Cerniglia said.

A Stranger Far from Home

Tomas Juonys, 1975–1999

MAY 26, 2002—A woodcutter's chance discovery one quiet Sunday afternoon outside of Black River Falls has turned into an international murder mystery that has puzzled local detectives— but drawn little interest from the public.

The skeletal remains found in February belong to Tomas Juonys, a Lithuanian immigrant who briefly and legally called Madison home more than two years ago. The town of Madison was his last residence, investigators say, before he died. The body lay in the woods near a Perkins restaurant fewer than one hundred yards off Highway 54, Jackson County Sheriff's Department Detective Susan Reshel said.

She won't say what killed Juonys but is confident the details of the cause of death will point toward homicide. The case has already led her to Illinois to interview a distraught father who came to this country from Klaipeda, Lithuania, specifically to look for his missing son. In Indiana, a half-brother may hold keys to the dead man's work history. American and Lithuanian embassies have become involved. Reshel won't say much about the case, and the details of Juonys's life here leave few clues. He seems to have been an almost anonymous immigrant.

Juonys, who was twenty-three or twenty-four years old at the time of his death in 1999, came to the United States in 1996 with a visa that would allow him to participate in a Hawaiian running race, the Honolulu City Lights Ultra Run, which is a race that can go on for fifty miles or more. There is no evidence he ever took part in that race, and photographs of Juonys do not show someone who appeared to be a long-distance runner.

Placing a name to the body, unofficially, three months ago was not that difficult. Found with the remains of the body were Juonys's Lithuanian passport, some papers, a billfold, tennis shoes, and a jacket. Reshel is waiting for DNA test results for an official confirmation of identity.

It appears that between 1996 and 1999, Juonys lived in Indiana and then Wisconsin, where he was listed as renting an apartment at 2701 Granada Way, which is officially in the town of Madison. The street, once a notorious haven for illegal drug sales, has since been somewhat rehabilitated and renamed Pheasant Ridge Trail.

Juonys secured a Social Security number while in Indiana. Reshel would not say if or where Juonys worked while in Madison, which is, coincidentally, the sister city of Vilnius, Lithuania.

After the remains were found, Reshel pieced together how Juonys happened to get to Black River Falls. A retired deputy recalled that an abandoned car was towed from a nearby motel, the Arrowhead Lodge, some time ago. A search of records discovered the towed vehicle was a brown 1990 Mercury Topaz sedan, registered to Juonys, who also had a valid Wisconsin driver's license. The motel is less than a mile from where the body was found, and Reshel discovered Juonys had stayed there for two days.

Juonys (pronounced: yoo-ah-NEES) was in the United States legally. His visa, issued for that ultramarathon, did not expire until November 2000, long after it is believed he was killed.

Reshel said the language barrier has made the investigation difficult, though "the Lithuanians I have met with have been very cordial, and the [Juonys] family connection is very strong."

Reshel had to set up, through the Lithuanian embassy, the sensitive task of telling Juonys's father that his son is dead. "They broke the news to the brother, and then the son contacted the father," she said. "They are wonderful people. You could tell the father was distraught. He wants the remains back, but we can't release them at this time."

Reshel said she plans to try to track down people in Madison who may have known Juonys and his background. She might also try the Wisconsin Dells area, where there is a Lithuanian presence and where Lithuanian youth have been recruited to work in the tourist industry for the past few years.

Nijole Etzwiler, a member of the Madison-Vilnius Sister City Committee, said her Lithuanian friends and acquaintances were curious about the case, which was reported with scant background two months ago as the finding of an unidentified body of a Lithuanian man.

Told of the identification, Etzwiler said Juonys may have been "what we sometimes call the Third Wave" of Lithuanian immigrants. "This happens too often. They get over here, the young ones, and they can get lost," she said. Most go to Chicago, which boasts the largest population of Lithuanians outside of that country. It would not surprise her, she said, if Juonys did not have any contact with other Lithuanians in Madison.

Police say there is no record of anyone reporting Juonys missing. Except for a town of Madison parking ticket in 1998, Juonys had no police record.

Pennies from Heaven

Myrtle Haywood, 1919–2002

DECEMBER 20, 2002—Myrtle Haywood, a self-professed psychic and Madison character who had the faith of a mustard seed and passed it along—usually taped to a penny—died Tuesday. She was eighty-three.

Haywood, a retired Oscar Mayer worker who ran the Sunshine Center of Light from her small home on Haywood Drive, told fortunes, gave readings, and informed strangers of upcoming events and illnesses.

In 1974, she began a spirited effort to raise money to pay for a park in Mount Horeb, her hometown. The park had already been built and named in honor of her mother, Agnes Foster. Haywood told fortunes—for donations of about fifty cents each, which she always donated to charity—using playing cards. To each person who listened to one of her readings, Haywood would give a penny with a mustard seed attached with a piece of cellophane tape.

The tiny mustard seeds—each with the ability to grow into a thirty-foot bush—were a reference to a Bible verse about faith. Haywood was a longtime member of St. Mark's Lutheran Church, at 605 Spruce Street in Madison. "The pennies mean something in terms of Momma," Haywood told reporter William Wineke in 1974. "My mother would never take anything from anyone. When she got old and couldn't open her own cans and jars, she'd take them to men down the street, but she always gave them a penny for their trouble."

After 1974, Haywood occasionally appeared in the news with updates on her adventures. She was an indefatigable self-promoter, traveled widely in pursuit of psychic interests, and managed to combine a desire to help others with a deep religious belief that faith could move mountains. "I think God gave me this ability to use to help people," she said.

Myrtle Haywood. J. D. PATRICK, *WISCONSIN STATE JOURNAL*

In 1998, at age seventy-nine, she earned the equivalent of a high school diploma, and held her graduation party at the Klinic Bar on Park Street.

As Wineke wrote in a "Myrtle update" in 1979, "She is the least likely psychic one could imagine. There is nothing mysterious about her; she lives in a small cluttered house with her husband, George. . . . She talks a mile a minute, flits from one subject to another, jumps feet first into areas where angels would demand safety nets and hard hats, and seems to have a marvelously good time no matter where she is or what she is doing."

Her good cheer was infectious. For just that part of her life, and for representing a quirky but well-meaning portion of this community's population that seems to be dwindling, there are many who will miss her.

The Girl Who Survived

Anita Kayachith, 2001–

MARCH 11, 2003—The cause of the crash was slippery conditions. The semitruck was westbound at 4:15 a.m. when it went out of control, jackknifed in its own lane, kept going across the median, and crossed the eastbound lane, where it clipped the Honda and came to rest in the far ditch.

Two adults in the Honda were dead at the scene. The truck driver fared better but, in the dark, snowy conditions, was not even aware that his truck had hit anyone. So he did not see a little pink-clad passenger walk away from the smashed car and toddle off into the cold, snowy morning darkness. Her stocking feet left footprints in the new snow on the two eastbound lanes of Interstate 94. Dawn was coming, and she was still sleepy.

When Rhonda Waldera eased her unmarked Wisconsin State Patrol car on to the snow-slippery Interstate Highway 94 before 6 a.m. last Friday, it was the start of another day at the office. A car was crushed, the top sliced off beneath a semitrailer, the passengers dead. Waldera had been pulled from her warm bed twelve miles away to help at the scene northwest of Black River Falls, with an eye on crash reconstruction.

But it was Waldera the mother, not Waldera the veteran trooper, who puzzled over the contents of the back seat of the topless 2000 Honda in the median. From what was there, she could tell something, or someone, was missing.

"I went up to the car with the coroner and began to conduct my investigation, looking at the parts of the car, the items in the car, things like that," she recalled. "I saw some things that would have been a kid's. Little shoes, a sippy-cup."

The shoes were blue, tiny. In the wrecked car, Waldera also saw some "pull-ups," or what parents might call "big-girl diapers." There was a child-sized suitcase, a little computer-type game. All were familiar items to Waldera and her husband, Duane, a Jackson County sheriff's detective, who have two children. Zach is five, and Danyelle is two. "I just started noticing all these things that you just don't normally leave in your car. I asked another officer where the little kid was."

But no one else besides the couple in the car had been found. Killed when their car went under the semitrailer were Souvorachak Kayachith, twenty-one, and his wife, Melinda Athakhanh, twenty, of Brooklyn Park, Minnesota.

By 6 a.m., the crash scene was filling with people—from the county highway department, the funeral home, the coroner's office, the Jackson County Sheriff's Department, and the State Patrol. One of the workers, in response to Waldera's observation, said he had noticed a doll by the semi, hundreds of feet away.

"We just started pursuing it more," Waldera said. "We were looking for anything, the possibility of anyone in the area. It was still dark, and we searched mainly the areas between the car and the semi. We didn't find anything."

In the dark as the snow continued to fall, at first no one searched much beyond the median, in the ditch. As the day dawned, traffic was rerouted, the scene cleaned, and Waldera persisted.

"One of the highway workers happened to see a bright pink [piece of clothing] over in the trees on the eastbound side," Waldera said. "We were on the eastbound side but in the median. The officer with me, Sean Berkowitch, went over there and found her and woke her up."

He woke up two-year-old Anita Kayachith, who did not cry. Coatless, in her stocking-feet, she sat in the snow and waited. Whisked by ambulance to Black River Falls Memorial Hospital, she had a scratch on her head and was back in the Twin Cities with relatives by Monday.

It wasn't until after they found the girl that officers spotted her footprints and backtracked, following them from the ditch, back up the embankment, across two lanes of the interstate, and to the car. Officials suspect she had been asleep in the back seat when the crash occurred. "She walked a couple hundred feet at least," estimated Waldera.

Anita was not wearing heavy clothing, and her coat and little blue tennis shoes were still in the car. She spent almost three hours in below-freezing temperatures and snow.

"I kept telling the others, we need to keep our options open. Don't close that option that there might be someone out there," she said. And no one, not one of the others at the scene, gave up, she said. "We were out there doing our job, just like we do every day on the Interstate."

But she says she knew that there was someone else there. "I don't know, to me it was second nature. You don't leave those things in the car. The sippy cup."

Waldera did not see the child when she was taken away, but she went to the hospital later Friday. She needed to get the girl's name for the reports. "I peeked at her. She was sleeping. She was very cute."

Captain Arne King credited the whole crew with finding the girl, and he credited Waldera for her persistence to keep everyone looking.

"She urged everyone on. She said there's got to be a little one around here someplace."

Waldera, thirty-one, six months pregnant, was back on the road Monday.

By the Way, You're Dead

Don Johnson, 1923–2013

NOVEMBER 30, 2003—In a rare turnabout example of the traditional next-of-kin notification, Fonda Johnson recently informed her husband, Don, of Stoughton, that he was dead.

Donald Burnell Johnson assured her he was very much alive, but she pointed to their monthly bank statement, which showed the Social Security Administration had taken back his October and November direct-deposit checks. The reason: He is deceased.

He is because the Social Security Administration (SSA) says so.

Fonda Johnson called the SSA to tell them he was alive, and the SSA suggested she drag him down to the local office to prove it. "Fortunately, the SS teller at window No. 3 was a high school friend of our daughter, so she pushed some buttons and said, 'Now you are resurrected,'" Don said.

But once those wheels are in motion, they are hard to stop.

"We got a call from St. Mary's, where I had a gallbladder operation last September, saying their Medicare claim has been denied because I am deceased," he said.

Don, at eighty and after a long career in Madison as a structural engineer for Mead & Hunt, is feeling quite healthy, though his buddies these days keep asking, and it's been hard to convince Uncle Sam of that.

"Last week my wife got this nice red, white, and blue pamphlet and a letter notifying her that the new check has already been deposited in her name," Don said.

The letter began: "You are entitled to monthly widow's benefits . . ." There was a bonus, too. "A one-time $255 worker's death benefit had been added to the amount."

That was one official notice too many. An 800 number was included on that form if the widow had any questions. She called.

"They wanted to talk with me if I was available," Don said. "I answered all the usual questions, and the computer indicated there was an error but couldn't say how long it would take to straighten out."

He suspects another Don Johnson, somewhere, may be the actual late Don Johnson, although their different Social Security numbers should have prevented any confusion. The mix-up might also be related to the postal addresses the Johnsons use, split between Wisconsin and Florida.

As of last Wednesday, the government had returned the money it had withdrawn from the couple's Florida bank savings accounts but had not moved to take back the money paid to Fonda Johnson as widow benefits. "I talked with three offices, and they all say just wait and they will try to get it fixed. They don't have a program that fixes it, I guess."

It was a lot easier back in 1942, when Don signed up for Social Security. "I got my number when there was a Social Security office in a little old house on Wisconsin Avenue, where the City-County Building is now. I was a student, and went to work for Badger Ordnance and had to get a number. That was in 1942."

In 2003, however, it's a little less personal. "We got one letter from Chicago that wasn't signed, saying they were working on it," he said. Then another, from Baltimore, also unsigned, saying never mind, but they are still working on it.

He suspects his death notice may have something to do with his gallbladder operation, though officials at St. Mary's Hospital said they made no notification to the government about it. "My lawyer said maybe somebody in the government thought I wasn't going to make it," he joked.

His buddies at the Madison West Rotary Club have been having some fun with his official status. "And I have been getting a strange feeling that I am invisible," he added.

His family has a history of mysterious—to the SSA anyway—deaths. "It all reminds me of when my dad died at [the] age of eighty-eight. He had direct deposit of his Social Security checks, and they couldn't get his checks stopped," he said.

Johnson is taking his exaggerated demise fairly calmly and with good humor. In Chicago, however, officials are a little embarrassed. "Yes, we do have this on our radar screen," assured Doug Nguyen, regional public affairs specialist. "We have let our Wisconsin public affairs office know that this erroneous death report has occurred."

According to Nguyen, such errors are rare. He estimated their occurrence at less than 1 percent. "A whole slew of [death reports] come in, and what we do normally is verify that those death reports are accurate. Except when [it comes from] an immediate family member, [then] we assume they are correct," he said.

Once a person is on the Social Security record as living, breathing, and receiving benefits, and that person gets mistakenly terminated—with a capital letter *T* put in the record—it is difficult to resurrect the person, however alive that person may be. "We still have to verify that he is alive," he said. "Believe me, we know it causes hardships, and in those cases, we do have emergency payment procedures."

But how did Johnson get inaccurately terminated in the first place? Though Johnson said he has been told "we'll never know," Nguyen said if the SSA finds out, they'll tell him. And if Johnson wants to know, he has the option of going to the SSA office and having someone track that information down for him.

And he should be ready to get some more mail. "Once the record is revitalized, he will get some notices. He will get lots of notices," Nguyen said.

According to the SSA website, of the 2.3 million people who die in the United States each year, about 2 million were receiving SSA benefits.

Though the SSA receives reports of death from a variety of sources, about 90 percent of deaths are reported by friends, relatives, and funeral homes. Postal authorities and financial institutions report another 5 percent of deaths. SSA relies on computer matches with federal and state agencies to identify the remaining 5 percent of deaths.

Johnson said it doesn't appear the SSA notified anyone but himself of his death.

"They haven't reported it to my insurance company yet. I thought maybe I would be getting a big check," he said.

Don Johnson lived another ten years beyond his first "death." He died in 2013 at the age of eighty-nine.

Prolific Letter Writer

Elmer F. Cox, 1912–2003

DECEMBER 23, 2003—Elmer F. Cox, a hearing aid salesman with an irresistible urge to share the results of an unquenchable curiosity, usually in letters to the editor, died Friday at age ninety-one in a Madison hospital.

He wrote many letters to Madison newspapers, taught patriotism and flag-waving etiquette, campaigned against such injustices as clunky post office mail drawers, and once accepted a hot dog from actress Marlene Dietrich. He was somewhat of a self-taught expert on song copyrights and was a virtual encyclopedia on the history and uncopyrightability of the song "Happy Birthday."

Cox had a roundabout way of getting to a point, but the journey was usually interesting. In 1980, he wrote to the editors of the *Guinness Book of Records*, noting that "we have a large POST OFFICE in Madison, Wisconsin, USA, a City of 180,000 persons, that I believe is the only one in the World that does not have a slot to mail a letter."

That was Cox's way of protesting the fact that post offices here required patrons to deposit letters in a "bin" rather than a "slot," the former requiring the sender to grasp a handle and pull open a drawer, into which is placed the envelope. Cox insisted he was not against bins. He was simply against the absence of slots.

Cox, a World War II and Korean War veteran who worked in

medical units, was also slyly pointing out that a disabled person would have difficulty with a bin but not with a slot. He saw no reason both could not be offered.

Several years ago, in a feature article about D-Day and the Normandy Invasion, Cox recalled helping evacuate casualties, often flying over the English Channel in planes loaded with ammunition, then returning with the same planes filled with injured soldiers. On one of his last trips to Germany, actress Marlene Dietrich, working on a Red Cross truck, gave him a hot dog.

While Cox's opinions leaned to the conservative side, his letters to the editor were on all sorts of topics. One day he might be praising the University of Wisconsin–Madison crew team, and the next he would be lamenting the complicated return envelopes provided by utility companies. He flirted with local politics in the 1970s, running for the Madison Common Council in an east side district while urging the city, "Do not let Madison, Wisconsin, become a Berkeley, California."

Cox attended classes at UW–Madison as a special student after retirement and seemed to enjoy learning

Elmer Cox, pictured in 1993. L. ROGER TURNER, *WISCONSIN STATE JOURNAL*

things. He was sometimes (politely) surprised when the logic of his observations was not greeted with the same enthusiasm with which it was offered. Brevity, however, brought him as much as or more attention than logic, and his short opinions were frequently published.

The Lenient Police Chief

James Bjork, 1928–2004

AUGUST 19, 2004—James E. Bjork, bowling alley proprietor, part-time Cambridge police chief, chauffeur to a very rich woman, and a "really good tickler," died Monday.

Bjork, seventy-five, and his wife, Mary, ran the Old Bowling Alley and Jim and Mary's Bar in Cambridge. Before then, Bjork worked for a propane gas company and served as Cambridge's entire police department from 1968 to 1975.

It was daughter Elaine May who remembered her dad Tuesday as "a really good tickler."

"He was pretty lenient," May said. "There were no really big police cases back then, but a lot of people have already commented about how they remember him giving them a ride home after they had one too many."

Bjork quit law enforcement in 1976 when he and his wife opened Jim and Mary's—"nothing fancy," May said. Bjork's father also was in the bowling alley business, Mary Bjork said.

It was after he came home from the Korean War that a friend "fixed him up with a job as the chauffeur for Mrs. Parker," of the Parker Pen family in Janesville, Mary said. He didn't tell stories about those days driving Mrs. Parker—no one could remember her first name, and the pen company archives were unclear on the identification—but he lived at the Parker residence, coming home for two days weekly.

"That was before my time," she said. She and her husband got together after he had already met her sisters and "he picked what was left," she said, laughing. They married in 1961, and her four children—all Rileys—were joined by three Bjorks, totaling four daughters and three sons, all surviving.

Busy till the End

Sylvester Klinkner, 1920–2004

SEPTEMBER 29, 2004—Sylvester Klinkner, eighty-four, died Friday. A thirty-eight-year employee of Oscar Mayer Foods, he was an accomplished ham-boner, capable in his prime of boning sixty picnic hams in an hour.

He had his hips replaced three times and, staying active in retirement, fixed up and sold many used bicycles to children from the neat garage of a Midvale Boulevard home he shared with Dorothy, his wife of fifty-eight years.

Searching for something to keep himself busy, Klinkner decided in 1992 to fix bicycles, though he had never so much as changed a wheel spoke in his life. His first year, he bought, fixed, and sold three bicycles, but eventually he would sell up to one hundred repaired bicycles in a summer.

A little more than a year ago, the Klinkners' home was invaded by two brutal robbers who attacked and beat both Klinkner and his wife, stealing a checkbook and credit cards. Though not seriously hurt, police said, the couple experienced restrictions in their lives because of the crime.

Recently, two men, Ronald Gabel and Thylonius Edwards, were sentenced to prison for fifteen and twenty years, respectively, for their parts in several robberies, including the attack on the Klinkners.

Sylvester Klinkner puts a new tire on a Schwinn bicycle in his garage repair shop in 2003. JOHN MANIACI, *WISCONSIN STATE JOURNAL*

In a column in the *Wisconsin State Journal* in 2003, Klinkner—whom everyone called "Syl"—said he had slowed down considerably, fixing about one bicycle per day.

He liked to sit in his garage, munching one of his wife's oatmeal chocolate-chip cookies and chatting with passersby. "I can sit out here and have a can of pop, and people stop by to visit. It's better than sitting in the house and watching TV—I'd go nuts."

He said his favorite bicycle brand was a Schwinn, "one of the old ones."

He is survived by his wife and a daughter, Patricia Seaman.

Casualty of War

Mark Maida, 1982–2005

JUNE 2, 2005—Mark Maida still makes them laugh. That was what he brought to the party, to the family, even to the war. He brought the fun. Now he makes them cry, too.

"He always wanted to make sure we weren't hurting. He wanted to show us that, 'Look, hey, I'm okay,' " said Betsy Jacobs, Mark's girlfriend. "There were times he said it was hard for him, but he knew it was harder for us because we didn't know what was going on."

Mark, twenty-two, a 2001 graduate of Memorial High School, died last week in Iraq. He was a crew member on a Humvee on night patrol in Diyarah when a homemade bomb exploded, killing him and wounding two other crew members. He had just been promoted to sergeant with the US Army's Second Squadron, Eleventh Armored Cavalry Regiment.

"He was counting the days, the hours. He had a lot of dreams," Betsy said.

Wednesday afternoon, led by parents Ray and Diane Maida, family and friends continued to tap a well of memories of their friend, brother, and son.

They brought out the goofy photos Mark sent back from Iraq, wearing bunny ears at Easter, cooking marshmallows over a tiny stove. They remembered him "coming through Madison like a hurricane" on leave from assignment in the Mojave Desert. They shared lots of photographs, lots of pictures of Mark smiling.

"With Mark, we didn't have to work that hard to have fun, not with him around," Ray said.

And they continued, quietly but firmly, not wanting to spoil the message of their love for their son and what he was and could have been, to question the support the government gives its troops at war and the military policies that circulate soldiers beyond their tours of duty.

The Maidas have a unique viewpoint on this family tragedy. Mark was the youngest of four children, all Memorial graduates who grew up in the Orchard Ridge neighborhood of Madison.

Ray, a retired Madison police detective, is a Vietnam War combat veteran. Diane is a nurse at UW Hospital. Mark's brother Chris, twenty-four, is a former member of the Madison-based Golf Company, one of 172 US Marine reservists who returned in April after ten months in Iraq. For a time, Chris, now on inactive

reserve, was stationed twenty miles from his brother in what Ray called the "triangle of death south of Baghdad." His fellow Marine and best friend, Robert Warns, of Waukesha, was among the casualties from that unit.

A sister, Juliann Mutch, thirty-one, and brother, Aaron, twenty-eight, recalled their brother as "one of the little guys, always happy," who wrote his nieces and nephews funny letters and who was himself just becoming old enough to share the "old ones" family fun.

Sergeant Mark Maida.
COURTESY OF DIANE MAIDA

Diane answers for the family when she is asked if there is a message in her son's death. At the hospital, "when we see young people die, we are always looking for an organ donor," she said. "Mark couldn't be an organ donor. I want his death to have some meaning for others."

Their son had talked about the difficulty in maintaining vehicles and the lack of time available for such important tasks, Ray recalled.

"It is folly to say, 'We support our troops,' when we're not giving them what they need for equipment. Our cars here have yellow ribbons of support for the troops, but there are not enough soldiers to fight this war. At this point, it doesn't seem like a goal that can be accomplished," he said.

Mark's enlistment—three years spent in the States—was to have ended October 31, 2004, after his brother was sent to Iraq. But due to the military's policy of allowing up to ninety days to order a recall, he was not discharged.

The policy is unfair, said Juliann, who has written to politicians to protest it. The feeling was echoed by her parents, who said it is evidence the burden of the war is not being shared equally. Ray said on Wednesday the family received a letter, dated May 18, from Mark that included his own objections to the policy.

Instead of returning to Madison, moving in with his girlfriend, and enrolling at Madison Area Technical College to study electrical engineering, he was kept in the army. He went to Iraq with his mechanized infantry unit in January.

"For Mark, being there had nothing to do with ideology," said his brother, Aaron. "His concern was for watching out for his friends. He was not a violent person."

Ray remembered receiving the news last Thursday night, after he and his wife and son Chris went out to eat and listen to an Irish band. "It was about ten p.m., and I went in to the bedroom to lie down. Diane went to get a book to read. She came back in and said, 'There's a man in a uniform at the front door, and he has to talk to both of us.'"

The message was brief, the sorrow immediate and inescapable.

"I didn't want him to leave," Ray said.

"I kept asking him to please stay here. I kept touching him, I kept grabbing at his coat."

Heiress of the Big Top

Sally Clayton-Jones, 1937–2005

AUGUST 20, 2005—Salome "Sally" Juliar Ringling Clayton-Jones, sixty-eight, granddaughter of one of the original Ringling Brothers and patron of the local arts and Circus World Museum, died at her Baraboo home Friday.

Her name was never on a marquee at a performance of the Greatest Show on Earth, but she lived life in capital letters. Even so, her friends and family said she was more interested in talking quietly about you than about herself.

"She would like to have her hands in every pie she could put her hands in," said son Charles Clayton-Jones, of Baraboo.

Always called Sally, Clayton-Jones grew up in Baraboo, where her ancestors the Ringling Brothers—first five, then two more—began a tented circus in 1884 that became in 1907 the "Greatest Show on Earth." Her father was Henry Ringling, son of the youngest of the Ringling Brothers, who was also named Henry. Sally was named after her great-grandmother Salome Juliar, mother of all seven original Ringling brothers.

Sally left Baraboo for a boarding school in Massachusetts when she was fourteen and did not return to live permanently in the family home on Eighth Street—built in 1900 for Charles Ringling—until her mother's death in 1992.

She then picked up where her mother, Jean Fowler Ringling,

left off as a supporter of the museum—the former quarters of the
Ringling Brothers Circus in Baraboo that now serve as the Wisconsin
Historical Society's Circus World Museum—and a multitude of
other area charities and causes.

"She was committed to a broad spectrum of interests," recalled
Dave SaLoutos, a Baraboo native who is the current ringmaster
and performance director at the museum. "She had a way of making
everyone comfortable, welcome. Entertaining was easy for her,"
he said.

She hosted a Christmas party and a big summer party and
"loved a lavish party," son Charles said. "There were no dancing
bears or anything like that, but lots of booze and tons of people.
She was a great cook. She traveled the world and collected recipes
from everywhere she went."

When her father, a physician not involved with the circus, died
in a car accident, she moved with her mother and brother to Rome.

"She got a job as a translator for Maserati, and through those
connections she met a lot of Formula One race-car drivers,"
said Charles.

She became engaged to legendary German driver Wolfgang
von Trips, who died—along with at least thirteen spectators—
in a 1961 crash racing his Ferrari at Monza. Her devotion to
motorcar racing and knowledge of Italian, said Charles, earned
her the respect of drivers and mechanics on the race-car circuits
that evolved into Grand Prix racing.

Sally earned a nickname: "Gearbox." She was often asked to hold
tools while the cars were being worked on, he said, which prompted
a suggested epitaph: "She never said 'No,' to 'Here, hold this.'"

As a Ringling—thanks to the circus, one of the richest families
in the country in the 1900s—she moved in elite, jet-set circles.
In 1962, that brought her to St. Moritz, where she met her husband,
William Clayton-Jones, a "dashing RAF pilot," according to Charles.
The pilot tried to budge her out of a bobsled ride with Prince

Michael of Kent. She protested—the prince had just offered her a ride—and he offered to make up for the gaffe with dinner.

The couple moved to Jamaica, but Sally and the family fled to London when the politics of that country made it dangerous, Charles said. Then her husband—who had taught Sally how to fly—died in a plane crash in Jamaica, at the age of forty-two.

The death reintroduced a familiar, tragic element of the Ringling family, notes circus historian Fred Dahlinger. "They have a kind of, I wouldn't really call it a curse, but Henry [Ringling Sr.] died relatively young, and Henry junior [Sally's father] died prematurely in a car accident, and her brother died young. They have had that experience with early loss of life in the family, and Sally was also relatively young," Dahlinger said.

In London, Sally began a career that started with cooking in the cafeteria as a way of getting her foot in the door of a London auction house, where she worked her way to a position crisscrossing Europe. "Based in London, going back and forth to Rome, she traveled around looking for old race cars, Formula Ones and Formula Twos, persuading car collectors to trade up," Charles said.

Sally's daughter, Mary Catherine (called Kate), said she "gave me really big footsteps to fill. She taught me that as a woman you can do anything."

Kate is an airline pilot and recently earned an MBA from the University of Massachusetts. "She challenged me. She would share her success stories and the way she did it, and I came to understand that it was her way to give me examples of what can be done," she remembered. "She had the tools, the social graces, and the intelligence to really go up. She spoke five languages fluently; she had all the European communication tools. Her second language was Italian. After she had her stroke, she spoke better Italian than English."

The stroke, in 1997, slowed but did not stop her activities in Baraboo, where she became the latest Ringling to take up the mantle of patron in this historic city.

While the Ringlings were a family of spectacle to the public, to their descendants they were just family, said Kate, who with her brother Charles spent summers in Baraboo with their grandmother. "As kids, with the Circus World Museum in our backyard, it was where we went to summer camp, it's how we played as kids. We weren't trapeze artists, but we played with tiger cubs," she remembered.

"When we look at our Ringling history, it is very private. What normal people look at as spectacle, to us these are the stories and photographs that fill our house. The fact that our family tried to build an airplane and use Eighth Street as a runway is not only a story, we still have the tools they used to build the airplane," she said.

To those who knew her personally, Sally too was more than her famous family name. "She was above the gossip of the family," said Merlin Zitzner, who heads Baraboo National Bank, which has shepherded Ringling fortunes great and small since "the beginning of Ringling time." He described his friend Sally as "a fun-loving gal, an extraordinary person with an extreme desire to carry on the family tradition."

"She was rich and colorful, but colorful in the sense of the passions of life," he said. "You wouldn't get bored talking with her. Wherever traditionalists would reach out for nostalgia, she would be there with a real experience."

By living, and dying, in Baraboo, Sally continues another Ringling tradition particular to her line in the family, noted Dahlinger.

"The elder Henry was one of the two Ringling brothers who really stuck it out in Baraboo. He had a great love of books and arts, and it seems like that kind of passion for those aspects of life were found in Sally's own. That was an excellent part of Sally's character, her interest in arts, life, and human creative endeavor," he said.

Almost Famous

Carl Thayler, 1933–2005

NOVEMBER 10, 2005—One of Madison's most successful unknown poets, Carl Thayler, was found dead of natural causes Sunday in his small apartment a few blocks off Park Street.

He was seventy-two and leaves family in California, several books of sometimes contrarian, sometimes lyrical poetry, and an unfulfilled desire to buy a candy-apple red Harley.

Thayer's poetry was published in several books and small press journals, including *Skanky Possum*. He taught poetry, survived poverty and poetry critics, race car driving, an acting career in which he was touted as the "next James Dean" (a friend of his), dates with movie and television star Loretta Young, heart bypass surgery, and a liver transplant.

In the 1950s in his native California, Thayler was a movie actor, rugged, curly haired, handsome, but destined for smaller, supporting roles in B-movies. He played Robert Ford, the coward who shot Jesse James in the B-movie classic *The True Story of Jesse James*. He also appeared in *The Abductors*, *The Man from Del Rio*, *High School Confidential*, and others.

"He was very gentle, passionate about his beliefs," said Deborah Katz Hunt of Oregon, a former sister-in-law of Thayler.

An admirer of country-western music and iconic poet Ezra Pound, Thayler moved to Madison in 1968 with his then-wife,

Marcia, to attend graduate school in philosophy. Their daughter, Emily, was born in Madison. In 1969, he also had his first book of poetry published, a limited edition *The Drivers* by Perishable Press in Mount Horeb.

"He didn't finish his PhD because he just wanted to write poetry," Katz Hunt said.

Between 1968 and his death last week, Thayler lived away from Madison only six or seven years, including while studying writing and teaching at Bowling Green State University, and a couple of years living in a trailer in northern California.

Marcia Wolf, his former wife, said Thayler's acting life in the 1950s was preceded by study in New York and a friendship with James Dean.

Not a great actor, but a memorable one, might have been a description of Thayler in his Hollywood years. An interviewer at the time said Thayler had "all the bad manners but none of the talent of James Dean," recalled Wolf.

His poetry, she said, was "very intellectually demanding, very complex." He often spent twelve hours a day writing short stories, essays, and poetry. "He wrote the way other people breathed. Among a certain set of poets, he was well known and respected."

His poetry has been described as part of the Black Mountain poets, a school of poetry associated with writers of the 1930s and 1940s at Black Mountain College, South Carolina. One of the best known of those poets, Edward Dorn, is quoted in a blurb on Thayler's impenetrably titled *Poems from Naltsus Bichiden*, a publication of Skanky Possum: "Very hard examples, the eternal scratch of the pen. The language necessary to effect such concentration would require that you be eternally alive and slightly inverted, and Carl Thayler's got it."

Thayler had a heart attack on Christmas Eve in 1986 and had numerous related health problems since. An interviewer, excerpted on Thayler's website, noted Thayler's medical problems and asked him about poetry's relationship with death. "To this particular poet it means I am invulnerable," Thayler said. "I've seen my life through that dark glass a few times when there was a slim chance of waking the following day, and there wasn't a regret."

Actually, there was, according to Thayler's friend, the poet Howard McCord, a professor at Bowling Green and the man who alerted police Sunday when Thayler didn't answer his phone.

Though he finished his coursework for a doctorate in philosophy at the University of Wisconsin–Madison, the death of a friend, poet Paul Blackburn, led him to commit to poetry.

"He felt it carried him far beyond where philosophy was leading him," McCord said. "So he gave up his wife and his child and went off to be alone and a poet, which he regretted. It was a very high price to pay for poetry."

Pagan Suicide

Hilary Karnda, 1941–2005

DECEMBER 10, 2005—Hilary Karnda, a holistic healer and herbalist, told her friend on November 2 she was going to a sendoff at Wildcat Mountain State Park, and she needed a ride. She didn't tell her friend she was going away to die.

The only clues investigators had to who she was were some pagan symbols found with her body, discovered by hunters in the woods off Highway 131, in the park but not along a trail, on Thanksgiving Day.

Karnda, sixty-four, died of exposure to the Wisconsin November cold, Vernon County Sheriff Gene Cary said Friday.

"There was no indication of fatal illness, and nothing to indicate she had any heart disease or cancer," Cary said.

She just started listening to her tape recorder, prepared a place beneath an oak tree, and let nature take her.

It took more than three weeks for investigators to piece together evidence linking the death to a pagan ceremony, then to Karnda's connection with pagan or pagan-related groups, in an effort to identify the body, Cary said.

Karnda, who had lived in southern and southwestern Wisconsin, including Madison, most of her life, had been living in a small apartment in Richland Center and before that in rural Muscoda. Authorities had not yet been able to contact her relatives Friday.

Karnda described herself in the *Wisconsin Healer Pages*, a directory of holistic healers, as an herbalist and natural healer with "twelve years' experience in the medical field" and a "Master Herbalist degree from the Wisconsin School of Natural Healing."

Before identifying her, investigators thought the unidentified woman was drawn to the scenic state park to die because of a nearby American Indian burial site. Foul play was not suspected, county deputies said in November.

The circumstances remained mysterious Friday, though the sheriff issued a statement saying investigators, after being told by Ho-Chunk authorities that the ritual was not Native American, contacted "an expert on cults." That person, who "did not want to be named," confirmed the connection with a pagan belief system.

Paganism, which has various definitions rooted in a love for and kinship with nature, has adherents throughout Wisconsin. Cary would not say how Vernon County chose its expert.

"We plugged her in with what we had, and the first thing [the expert] asked was, 'Was the body at the base of an oak tree?' And it was. And she said, 'This is what you have: It is pagan, and you may want to try A, B, or C,'" Cary said.

Among other clues, investigators found with Karnda a five-pointed star, a leather pouch or medicine bag adorned with unspecified symbols, and a necklace. Either a cassette or compact disc player—Cary didn't know which—was also found, with the batteries run down. "Once we charged that up, several things pagan were mentioned on that, too," Cary said.

There were "no identifying documents, no driver's license, no Social Security card, no letters or addresses, no medication bottles, none of that stuff. As far as a name, she didn't exist," said the sheriff.

"There is every indication she was alone when she died," said Cary, clarifying that she had not told her friends she was going to be alone. It appears she purposely misled the person who drove her to Wildcat Mountain State Park, saying she needed to meet some friends who were "going to perform a ceremony sending her off," Cary said.

"When this driver dropped her off, she had no reason to believe it wasn't going to be safe, and that she wasn't meeting her friends just over the hill," Cary said. In a profile she wrote for *Wisconsin Healer Pages*, Karnda described herself as focused on helping her "clients become self-sufficient with their own health care, learning about their bodies, various holistic approaches and techniques, and how to sense their needs." She described her goal for her clients as empowerment.

"I don't discuss disease, but rather health," she wrote.

Cook's Bewildering Death

Tyler Kremin, 1971–2006

APRIL 19, 2006—Tyler Kremin, who put the bisque into bar cuisine at the venerable Echo Tap & Grill at South Bedford and West Main Streets, was found dead in his van outside the bar last week.

Far from an anonymous grill cook, the amiable Kremin's mysterious death has puzzled colleagues, who depended on his skill and friendship, and customers, who wondered at his ability to make a good bowl of soup.

Kremin, thirty-five, a native of Waukesha, celebrated the University of Wisconsin–Madison hockey team's national championship April 8 at the Echo, a family-owned bar. He had been the cook there for about ten years.

He was scheduled to work the April 10 lunch shift. According to reports from the Dane County Coroner's Office and the Madison Police Department, when Kremin didn't show up, coworkers noticed his van and his car in the parking lot.

They looked in the van and saw nothing but at 8:30 p.m. decided to look again. When they saw what appeared to be a body in the back of the van, they contacted police. Fire rescue personnel forced open the door and found Kremin dead.

Coroner John Stanley said an autopsy showed no obvious cause of death, and police said the death does not appear to be suspicious.

After a toxicology report showed painkillers and alcohol in Kremin's system, Stanley ruled the death as accidental.

Lacking answers, coworkers and friends Tuesday reflected on their unexpected loss.

"Soups were his specialty," said Jon Uttech, bar manager. "He could make all kinds of soup here. This time of the year he made crawfish fresh asparagus bisque. People were already starting to ask for it. We didn't know where he learned to cook, he just loved doing it. He was real good at taking a look at three piles of stuff and making a lunch special out of it."

He also loved music and was a regular at concerts at the High Noon Saloon and bluegrass festivals.

"We all kind of sat back [after his death] and started thinking about anything that might have been troubling him. There were certainly no outward signs," Uttech said.

Kremin was healthy, said a friend, and drank and partied a normal amount for a man his age. He once broke both wrists in a fall when he stubbed his toe while standing on top of the bar.

Katy Albert, an Echo bartender, had an idea of how her friend started cooking.

After work, he would make her a grilled cheese sandwich and would cut it into four pieces. He told Albert that growing up, he cooked for his younger siblings and a sandwich cut into four pieces was easier for small hands.

Mrs. Achenbach's Arachnid

Eency, 1990–2007

JANUARY 18, 2007—Children at North Crawford Elementary School have been stopping by Sally Achenbach's room for photo ops with a spider carcass.

They want a lasting memento of their pal, Eency, a Mexican brown tarantula that died last month after seventeen years of being spoiled in Achenbach's kindergarten class.

News of the popular spider's death, announced in the weekly *Crawford County Independent*, moved a couple to donate their college son's tarantula, Harry, to the class.

"Harry's been to Marquette University, four years," Achenbach said. "I'm sure he'll do well here."

The late Eency was purchased by Achenbach for eight dollars at a Boscobel pet shop seventeen years ago. Hundreds of kindergartners have cared for her—at a respectable distance—and hunted grasshoppers and crickets for her.

"The children loved to watch it take hold and suck the juice out of them," Achenbach, a kindergarten teacher here for thirty-two years, said sweetly.

It was just before Christmas when her students noticed that Eency hadn't moved in several days.

"The children were sad," she said. "You could tell from the

abdomen she was dead. It was quite flat. We just talked about how old she was, and about that's what happens. They die."

What then happens, at least with five-year-olds, is they get out their microscope and magnifying glasses and examine the carcass, just as they did previously with the "molts," or the exoskeletons shed by the tarantula.

The students in this kindergarten, located just outside of Soldiers Grove, have had lots of pets.

"We incubate eggs every spring for chickens," she said. "We've had turtles, frogs from tadpoles, hamsters, rabbits. We've hatched ducks."

Eency, however, stayed. On vacations, he went home with Achenbach.

She said the new tarantula, which is about ten years old, was named Harry by his owner, Ryan Hozhauer, who had the spider as a pet while attending college. But some kindergartners want to name him "Eency Two."

Eency, who is now known as "Eency One," was not an adorable pet, but she did pay attention in class.

"The kids would be sitting on the rug listening or doing a project and [Eency] would come to the glass and start waving arms at us," she said.

Achenbach has been receiving visits from former students who want to see what's left of the tarantula. Some get their pictures taken. Others just want one last look. Eency's remains will stay in a Cool Whip bowl for inspection by future budding arachnologists.

Achenbach's description of the pet would be high praise for any kindergartner, especially one who spent seventeen years there:

"Eency was fun. She never bit anyone."

The Hand Balancer

Thaddeus Augustynowicz, 1922–2007

SEPTEMBER 12, 2007—The first and probably only man to do a handstand on Balanced Rock at Devil's Lake State Park was found dead in his Castle Rock Lake area home August 28.

Large in life and larger than life would be good descriptions of Thaddeus Augustynowicz, eighty-five, a man known to everyone around Castle Rock as "Moose." He was a Golden Gloves boxer, champion weightlifter, wrestler and diver, a soldier, and expert at standing on his hands in unusual places.

"He was just a big guy, a strong friendly guy," said Barbara Baker, who fondly remembered her longtime friend Tuesday.

Baker said officials believe Augustynowicz died of injuries received in a moped crash, though they were unable to find a crash scene. He apparently crashed on a road near where he lived, got back on the moped and motored to his home, where he managed to clean up and put on some bandages, but died of his injuries, Baker said.

"He was in great shape, still worked out on the weights every day," she said. According to Baker, Augustynowicz was forty years old when he performed his infamous handstand. A photograph of the death-defying exploit, accomplished in July 1961, is on display at the park, she said.

"I have folders and folders of all that information," she said.

"He won lots of diving awards, was runner-up for Mr. Wisconsin. He had whole rooms filled with medals and trophies," she said.

Augustynowicz started bringing his family to the Castle Lake area to camp many years ago, Baker said. Eventually, they bought a chunk of land, got a trailer, upgraded, and finally he and his late wife, Helen, got a retirement home and moved to the area for good from Milwaukee in 1988. He was a familiar figure, wrote Rhonda Siebecker, editor of the *Juneau County Star-Times*, walking, mushroom-hunting, bicycling, swimming, cross-country skiing, hunting, and fishing.

A son, Tom, said his father loved to climb the bluffs at Devil's Lake and was an avid hand-balancer. "He used to polka on his hands and was part of a hand-balancing team."

Knockout Punch

Ronald Schellinger, 1961–2007

NOVEMBER 27, 2007—Ronald Schellinger, forty-six, a hard worker with many friends, a man who loved to plow snow from the streets of Hartford, died after a single punch to his nose outside a Dodge County bar over the weekend.

Dodge County Sheriff Todd Nehls said Schellinger was punched by Tyson Lotz, twenty-six, of West Bend, at 12:30 a.m. Saturday outside Hauser's Hideaway on Highway P, about four miles east of Hartford.

"He was punched just once and fell down," said Nehls, adding that the fatal injury was not caused by the fall.

Schellinger was taken to a Hartford hospital, then transferred to a Milwaukee hospital, where he died Sunday afternoon.

Nehls said the two men apparently did not know each other.

"Their paths crossed going from bar to bar, from the bar across the street," Nehls said. "Words were exchanged, and the next thing you know, one guy is down. We are interviewing witnesses to find out what was said, what generated the punch."

Hauser's Hideaway was closed Monday. A bartender at the bar across the street, Rubicon Oasis, reportedly called authorities to report a man was injured, Nehls said. Bar patrons also detained Lotz until deputies arrived, the sheriff said.

Lotz was being held in the Dodge County Jail on suspicion of first-degree reckless homicide.

According to online court records, Lotz has a history of battery and disorderly conduct arrests and convictions in at least three counties dating to 1996. In 2002, he was twice convicted of battery in Washington County, sentenced to terms of ninety days and five months in jail, and in one case ordered to pay five thousand dollars to the victim's mother and an insurance company.

Schellinger was described by his supervisor at the City of Hartford's streets department, Darryl Kranz, as "a super guy, who would do anything for anybody."

"He was very well liked," said Kranz.

Schellinger ran a family farm for eight years in the Dodge County town of Herman before joining the city as an equipment operator thirteen years ago.

"He did all the things in the street department, asphalt, everyday duties," Kranz said. "But he really waited for the snow. What he loved the most was plowing snow."

He said the death weighed heavily on street crews Monday.

Getting into a fight would have been out of character, Kranz added. "I don't think I have ever known him to get into a confrontation with anyone about anything."

Schellinger was elected to the Herman Town Board in 2001 and served two two-year terms, said the town clerk, Diane Beine, who is a former classmate of Schellinger.

"He was a good guy, an all-around good guy," Beine said.

Schellinger is survived by a wife, a son, and two daughters.

Farmers' Market Perennial

Jim Salzman, 1950–2007

DECEMBER 4, 2007—Jim Salzman, whose brash tone and tanned torso helped him sell peppers and melons at the Dane County Farmers' Market for more than thirty years, died of a heart attack Friday in Clearwater, Florida.

Salzman, fifty-seven, of Fall River, claimed to have planted his first garden at the age of four, and by age nine he had a first-place award for his tomatoes at the county fair. He graduated from college and taught kindergarten in 1976 before taking up vegetable farming for good outside of Fall River.

At Pinckney and Mifflin Streets, across from the YWCA, his Jim's Greenhouse truck, piles of vegetables, and his booming voice were familiar Saturday sights and sounds. On warm market mornings, he was an unforgettable sight, bronzed from the sun, wearing gym shorts barely larger than a nail apron as he filled baskets with produce.

"Jim was a showman in the best tradition, not afraid to be outrageous," said Mary Carpenter, former director of the market. In the fall, he might dress up as a big pumpkin, and for a time, he dressed in a chicken suit to sell chickens.

"He was supremely gentlemanly and polite," Carpenter said. "And boisterous," she added.

In 2002, after experiencing four years of crop-damaging bad

weather, Salzman filed for bankruptcy and told the *Capital Times* that his ultimate goal in life was "to be a farmer who doesn't complain about the weather." He remained in business and was at his familiar corner in a downsized version this past market season.

Salzman traveled annually to Clearwater to sell Christmas trees. Survivors include two former wives and four children.

Life after War

Shigeru Nakahira, 1920–2007

DECEMBER 29, 2007—Shigeru "Shig" Nakahira was a good and helpful friend, a capable accountant for the state of Wisconsin, a member of a floating poker game among fellow Japanese Americans, an excellent bowler and golfer, and a quiet doer of good deeds.

He was also the second-youngest of six siblings and a widowed father whose family was torn apart after they were split between three concentration camps. He was a soldier wounded while fighting with a highly decorated Japanese American regiment in World War II, a veteran looking for a chance to use the GI Bill, and an expert pickler of white radishes.

Nakahira, eighty-seven, died a week ago at Oakwood Village in Madison. His obituary notes two sisters and numerous nieces and nephews as survivors. A memorial service through Cress Funeral Home is planned but not yet scheduled.

Paul Kusuda and Nakahira played "inflation poker" together with buddies for many years. "We would each kick in a dollar and we got ten dollars' worth of chips," Kusuda said.

According to Kusuda, his friend was an accountant for a Madison pharmacy for several years before joining the state Department of Revenue, retiring in 1986.

Kusuda said Nakahira seldom spoke of his World War II

service as part of the 442nd Regimental Combat Team, which was made up of mostly Japanese Americans.

It was one of the most decorated units in World War II, with a motto of "Go for broke." Nakahira joined on June 28, 1944, and was assigned to the unit, according to Go For Broke, a Japanese American veterans' organization. This was after spending eight months at the War Relocation Authority camp at Tule Lake, California.

His niece, Millie King, who lives outside Denver, said the family was split among three "WRA" camps.

According to the 442nd's history, four thousand men joined that regiment in April 1943, and fourteen thousand served in it throughout the war, "ultimately earning 9,486 Purple Hearts, 21 Medals of Honor, and an unprecedented 8 Presidential Unit Citations."

One of those Purple Hearts went to Nakahira, who fought in Italy. In a 1998 interview, after receiving the Kathryn Lee humanitarian award in Madison, he told the *Capital Times* he suffered shrapnel wounds to his thigh and right hand.

"I tried to get him to talk about it in a presentation" to a service group, Kusuda said, "but he said very little. He would talk about how hard it was but not about war experiences. He never mentioned getting wounded, either."

King said her uncle lived with her mother (his sister) after the war, while attending Northwestern University on the GI Bill, earning a degree in accounting. He married and moved to Madison, but in 1953, his wife of two months was killed and he was injured in a car accident, according to the 1998 interview.

Nakahira was a champion Madison bowler, competing in as many as four leagues at once. When he took over as secretary for the Madison Area Retired Bowlers Association, he turned its attention to charitable works, particularly to area food pantries.

Kusuda said his friend was an active member in the Wisconsin chapter of the Japanese American Citizens League.

The love of pickled radishes and the skills to make them may have come from his youth. According to King, her uncle had grown up on a farm.

"Once a year, he would go to a tree farm place where they had lots of homegrown vegetables, and he would buy pound after pound of white radishes," recalled Kusuda. "He would pickle them using a special formula. . . . He made superior product."

Misplaced Faith

Alvina Magdeline Middlesworth, 1917–2008

MAY 13, 2008—While the corpse of an elderly, devout supporter decomposed on a toilet in a one-bathroom rural Necedah home for two months, at least twenty-five checks were written on the Mauston bank account she shared with the woman charged with covering up the death.

The accused woman, Tammy Lewis, thirty-five, is one of about six living adherents of the Immaculate Conception Chapel. The group is a spinoff sect unsanctioned by any mainstream religion, a fact met with indifference by most in Necedah, long a mid-Wisconsin hotbed of confusing but enthusiastic spiritual seekers.

The mortal remains of one of them, Alvina Magdeline Middlesworth, ninety, were found in a house on Shrine Road by a Juneau County Sheriff's Department deputy last week.

The longtime town chairman said the leader of Lewis's church, Alan Bushey, was "a charlatan from the word go," and another priest in a nearby two hundred-member congregation in Necedah said Monday, "We steer clear of that man. No one takes him seriously."

Bushey, who will be fifty-eight Wednesday, and Lewis have been charged in Juneau County Circuit Court with two felony counts of causing mental harm to a child, with Lewis facing an additional misdemeanor charge of obstructing an officer when she allegedly attempted to deflect a deputy's search for Middlesworth.

The mental harm to a child charges stem from accusations that Bushey and Lewis predicted financial doom to Lewis's two children and threatened to send them to public school if they revealed a corpse was in the bathroom. According to the criminal complaint, Middlesworth had been an important financial contributor to the church.

The children have since been placed in foster homes.

A search warrant returned Monday noted Lewis had a joint account with Middlesworth at the Bank of Mauston's Necedah branch. Since the woman's death, the account received direct deposits of three $590 Social Security checks and two $510 annuity checks, and Lewis admitted paying bills through the account since the death.

Juneau County District Attorney Scott Southworth declined Monday to say who wrote the checks. He said additional counts could come this week or next. He said he has been in touch with federal prosecutors, who would handle Social Security violations.

Lewis was helping Middlesworth change clothes in the bathroom about two months ago when she died, the complaint said. Lewis said God told her if she prayed hard enough, Middlesworth would revive.

She also said her "superior," who is also her codefendant and bishop of the church, offered encouragement in that mission as he received "signs" from God that such a miracle was on the way. They even left the bathroom door open for the first three days, but then closed it, according to the complaint.

Before moving to Necedah, Middlesworth, whose husband, Fred, died in 1990, was a longtime member of St. Mary of the Valley Catholic Church in Monroe, Washington. Reverend Michael O'Brien, her former priest there, said he and others, after researching the Necedah group, tried to dissuade her from going. At first, he said, she agreed to stay put but then sold her home and belongings and moved—with the help of Lewis—in 2005.

"She left in 2005, and I believe Tammy [Lewis] came out and got her," O'Brien said.

He suspects Middlesworth, who would have been in her late eighties at the time, may have become interested in Bushey's church when she visited her sister in Wisconsin.

"When this business came up, some of her friends and myself did some looking on the Internet to find out what it was all about, and I also called the diocese [in La Crosse], and got the word it was not a legitimate Catholic church," O'Brien said.

"She kind of pretended she wasn't going to go, but quietly sold her home and moved everything out and took off," he said.

He said members of the church are sad about what happened to her but understanding that there was nothing more anyone could do in those circumstances. "She was a very nice woman and very sincere. You hate to see somebody get taken in like that," he said.

After moving, she wrote the priest a letter saying she bought a house and two and a half acres of land.

The issue of what she owned is somewhat of a tangle. Town Chairman Vince Marchetti said Monday the home where she was found dead is owned by the Middlesworth Life Estate and was purchased from the Hilltop Family Trust, of Hazelton, Iowa. Its value is assessed at $78,200.

A life estate is a way for a person to stay in their home and establish a surviving ownership. Tammy Lewis is apparently the recipient of that, said Daniel Berkos, who was appointed her lawyer Monday.

The Hilltop Family Trust also owns the church's chapel, a converted home at N10314 Queensway valued at $134,000.

A search of real estate records in Juneau County turns up another transaction made January 7, 2007, that transfers the property of Carol Newland, also on Shrine Drive, to Middlesworth, Lewis, Elizabeth Kohles, and Newland. The warranty deed appears to establish a survivorship for the property that ends with Lewis and is also called a life estate. Newland refused to comment, except to say, "God bless you."

Marchetti, the town chairman who lives a few houses away from the house where Middlesworth was discovered, called Bushey the leader of "a pseudo Roman Catholic operation" that was a spinoff of another group that started fifteen to twenty years ago that was served by a retired Catholic priest.

Declaring independence and calling himself a bishop, Bushey emerged at Immaculate Conception, Marchetti said. That was "about nine or ten years ago."

"He had some funny ideas about religion," Marchetti said, adding, "There is nobody objective about this. Everybody in Necedah has an opinion."

Bushey apparently had been married, and divorced from, a woman in Georgia. The woman's brother-in-law said the divorce was long ago and that she wasn't interested in talking about it.

Lewis and Bushey remained in the Juneau County Jail on Monday with bail set at fifty thousand dollars.

Lewis, who is also called Sister Mary Bernadett, lived in Union Center, New Lisbon, and Columbus over the past several years. Her husband is believed to be in Oklahoma, according to court records.

Berkos, her lawyer, said he has requested she receive a mental health evaluation, as "she obviously has some emotional issues right now."

The Diocese of La Crosse issued a statement Monday afternoon stating, "In the Necedah area, though many organizations and independent groups claim to be Catholic entities, only St. Francis parish is part of the Diocese of La Crosse and thus in communion with the Roman Catholic Church."

The Reverend David Sansone, of Our Lady of Victory Chapel, who called his church "traditional Catholic, with the traditional Latin Mass, but not affiliated with the Diocese of La Crosse," said

Monday of Bushey, "We steer clear of that man. We know he has created a lot of trouble."

Still, Sansone was worried about the media coverage of Middlesworth's death. "The media always presents people like us unfavorably," he said.

On the Cutting Edge

Jody Samson, 1946–2008

JANUARY 6, 2009—A guy who described himself as "a lizard in the snow" of Wisconsin, Jody Samson would sit at Sportsman's Bar and Grill on First Street in New Glarus, order the daily special, and wash it down with a Fat Squirrel, the pride of the nearby New Glarus Brewery.

To most in New Glarus, Samson was that guy.

To the rest of the world, Samson, who was found dead of pneumonia at sixty-two on December 27 in his workshop, was a legendary designer and maker of swords and knives. With a world following in sword and sorcery circles, Samson was lured to New Glarus from California in 2001 by the owners of Albion Swords. He set up shop in downtown New Glarus, called it The Far Side, smoked cigars, and exploited the collectability of old designs of swords and knives.

Co-owned by Howard and Amy Waddell, Albion is the largest producer of authentic swords in the United States. According to Howard, in the world of authentic swords and knives, Samson was among the top designers.

"We are walking around in a stupor," Amy Waddell said Monday, about the effect of Samson's death on the staff of artisans at Albion.

Green County Coroner Jan Perry said the death is not suspicious. Samson had been dead for about a day before he was found by Amy Waddell's brother Lars Hansen, also a sword designer for Albion.

"He had complained of cold-like symptoms for about a week," Perry said. "Someone saw the lights on in his workshop and found him dead."

Samson, who had no known survivors, was a workaholic, Waddell said, going to his shop from his Main Street apartment at about one in the morning daily to work.

"His legacy is huge. Nearly every sword maker we know was inspired by swords appearing in *Conan*," Waddell said. That would be the famous Samson-designed weapon from the 1982 movie *Conan the Barbarian*. In the movie, Conan, played by Arnold Schwarzenegger, wreaks vengeance on his enemies with Samson's sword.

Samson got his start making knives by hanging around the workshop of prolific knife maker John Wesley Cooper, in Burbank, California, in the early 1970s. Samson also was known for his work creating butterfly knives, a special type of folding knife.

His work commands top prices. A copy of the Atlantean Sword from *Conan the Barbarian* is listed at $2,775, Waddell noted, and he also wrote fantasy stories for which he designed swords.

Margaret Ryser, co-owner of Sportsman's Bar and Grill, found him to be a very nice guy. "This was his second home, he was so versatile and well-informed," she said.

A memorial written by fellow designer Leif Hansen described Samson's workshop, with its

Jody Samson displays a cutlass he designed. HENRY A. KOSHOLLEK, *CAPITAL TIMES*

smell of Swisher Sweet cigars, the sound of Zeppelin in the background, and black steel dust (which he called "the Devil's dandruff") everywhere from grinders.

"I've never met anyone as fiercely and tirelessly creative as Jody Samson," he wrote.

Survivor of War, Parenthood

David Brenzel, 1916–2009

JANUARY 19, 2009—David Brenzel survived forty months as a prisoner of war, but he was more likely to tell you about the week he lived through in 1970—when seven of his kids were teenagers at the same time.

"So not much can bother me," he was known to say when recalling the chaos of parenting that many teens.

Brenzel, a letter-writer of sly humor, a former gandy dancer, and father of nine, died last week at ninety-three.

The conditions Brenzel endured as a prisoner of war in the Pacific gave him nightmares for the rest of his life. "For Dave, the war is finally over," his family wrote in his obituary.

Brenzel only began describing publicly the horrors of the war after making a trip to the Philippines in the 1980s, said his wife of more than sixty years, Mary Agnes. He was taken prisoner after the fall of Corregidor Island in 1942, after which he endured forced labor and survived living below decks of the "hell ships" used to house prisoners before being repatriated a month after VJ day. When he returned, the US government paid him one dollar per day for his prison time, his wife said.

He spent thirty of his forty months of slave labor as a welder in a Mitsubishi shipyard refurbishing the Japanese Navy. The experience soured him for parades, since the prisoners had been "paraded" two and a half miles to work every day in Yokohama, and for Mitsubishi, a company name he often remarked brought flashbacks.

"We put in full days on empty stomachs, kept lively by guards carrying pick handles, which we referred to as vitamin sticks," he wrote.

He didn't talk with his family about his prisoner of war experiences.

"It was something the children didn't know about, growing up, until about the seven or eighth grades, when a teacher would tell them to ask your parent about where they were during the war," Mary Agnes said. "He had nightmares most of his life, but he would just say in the morning that 'I dreamt about the war last night.'"

Brenzel was the "writer, photographer, and cartoonist" for *Wisconsin Tax News*, a publication of the Public Expenditure Service of Wisconsin, for forty years. He was known for his rescue of snapping turtles, his split pea soup recipe, and his "ardent interest in garden rodents," his family said.

He also wrote many letters to the editors of the *Wisconsin State Journal* and the *Capital Times*, some with wry comments about his prisoner of war experience and others with a pixie-ish bent, such as how he was a gandy dancer, maintaining railroad tracks for the Milwaukee Road in the prewar days, and how he survived having seven teenagers at once for a week in the 1970s.

"He had a wonderful sense of humor," said his wife, who grew up across the street from her husband-to-be in Milwaukee. Her only brother married his only sister, she said. The couple lived in the village of Oregon for the past eighteen years.

For This Hamlet, It's Not to Be

Hamlet, 1995–2009

JANUARY 27, 2009—Hamlet, a porcine jester more on par with Yorick than his namesake, alas, also is dead.

The people noshing at the Cottage Grove Lions Club Groundhog Day breakfast Saturday might pause mid-forkful to briefly praise the late Hamlet, who died January 5, but they hardly knew him.

This would have been his eighth appearance at the special breakfast fundraiser. Instead, the gimmick, if not the pig, lives on, as Hamlet's ashes will be in attendance, and a memorial service will honor his shadowy contributions of the past seven years.

Arriving by limousine, Hamlet would be invited to search for his shadow, à la groundhog. Two striking differences set the Cottage Grove event apart from the more renowned Sun Prairie event. In Sun Prairie, Jimmy invariably arrived on February 2, Groundhog Day, while Hamlet always made his appearance on a Saturday, when more people could show up to buy breakfast. Oh, and Hamlet was a ninety-five-pound potbellied pig.

While his species is less well known for its theoretical weather-predicting abilities, Hamlet was nonetheless locally renowned and successfully promoted for his congeniality and availability. He was a ham of infinite jest even before the Lions Club pig gig, winning accolades at fairs and appearing at schools where principals

Hamlet. HENRY A. KOCHOLLEK,
CAPITAL TIMES

had to kiss a pig to pay off a bet. It was steady work and didn't require lipstick, for the pig anyway.

Kym Thompson bought Hamlet, then four weeks old, fourteen years ago for fifteen dollars from a Deerfield farmer.

Monday, still bereft at the loss of her companion, Thompson explained that Hamlet was escorted to the sty in the sky on January 5, when it became clear the pain of old age and arthritis was too much.

Litter- and leash-trained, and willing to do tricks for an Oreo, Hamlet also was a fabled flying pig, a rumor laced with veracity due to the pig's survival of the 2005 Stoughton-area tornado, which destroyed the Thompson home and property. Airborne or no, he landed, at least figuratively, on his hooves. The lucky pig also acquired new pig digs, called "Ham-elot," with four windows, a ceiling fan, a little fireplace, and pictures of other pigs on the walls, Thompson said.

"He was totally devoted, passionate, very loving," Thompson said.

The demise of Hamlet put the Lions Club in a tight spot, spokesman Jim Guy said, though Thompson said she's hoping to adopt another pig.

"Well, we got this groundhog breakfast coming up on Saturday morning and we didn't know what to do, and we had to be a little delicate about it," Guy said.

Everything depended on Thompson's approval, but she was up for a memorial and will bring Hamlet's ashes for the service. There will be a eulogy. Everyone will just have to look for their own shadows, alas, not Hamlet's.

His Days Were Numbered

George Wood, 1928–2009

OCTOBER 10, 2009—Last week, George E. Wood, eighty-one, got tired, found a place to sit down out of the rain, and died.

The nearest place happened to be a couch in the lobby of Witte Hall, at 615 West Johnson Street, on the University of Wisconsin–Madison campus.

When authorities released news of the death, they had not identified the man found at about four o'clock in the afternoon on October 1 in the busy dormitory. The discovery prompted a two-hour shutdown of the lobby, and several students complained in the campus newspaper about the intrusion and security breach.

On Wednesday, Wood was remembered during a small funeral service at Our Lady Queen of Peace Catholic Church, where he married Frances Kostka on August 27, 1966, which was also his thirty-eighth birthday. She survives him. They had no children, but an obituary in the paper this past weekend said he left many "loving cousins, family, and dear friends."

He graduated from UW–Madison with a master's degree in urban and regional planning and worked for the state of Wisconsin as an urban planner—in the Department of Local Affairs and Development, which is now the Commerce Department—until his retirement. His passions, a friend noted for Wood's obituary, were classical and jazz music.

How he got to Witte Hall last Thursday, and why, were mysteries solved in part by Kurt Karbusicky at the Dane County Coroner's Office. He said Wood died of natural causes and had come to the campus area—where his wife had worked as a librarian before retiring—to do some shopping.

It was raining that afternoon, and Karbusicky suspects Wood simply sought refuge in the lobby, sat down on a couch, and probably had a heart attack.

Wood had been shopping at the University Bookstore, where he bought a calendar.

Rambling Man

Cornelius Cooke, 1932–2009

DECEMBER 14, 2009—Cornelius Cooke, a lanky retiree who commuted between Florida and Madison for thirty years in the same dilapidated Winnebago, died Wednesday at St. Mary's Care Center.

Cooke, seventy-eight, grew up in Madison but retired from carpentry in Hawaii, where he bought the Winnebago that was to be his only retirement address.

He would arrive in Madison in the spring and park the vehicle, most of the time legally, on city streets or in parks, spending his days walking, reading, or sitting with crossed legs looking out over Lake Wingra. Wary of strangers, though he spent decades in public places, he did not avoid conversation so much as maintain a polite distance.

"The farther off we are from people, the better off we are," he said in a 1994 interview. At the time, his eighty-five-year-old mother, Patty Fontell, had also been living in the Winnebago for four years.

They moved the vehicle often, used public restrooms but made no mess, created no disturbances, and accepted no welfare.

Virtually everything Cooke owned was under constant repair, from his spectacles to his bamboo stool perch inside the Winnebago to the vehicle itself, a collection of peeling veneer, wired or taped

Cornelius Cooke. PHOTO BY RICHARD
GEIER, *WINNEBAGO MAN*, 2009

connections, and loose parts. His mother died in 1997, but he kept on alone, parking at Walmart in Naples, Florida, for the winter and preferring a spot between Vilas Park and the UW Arboretum between May and October. Over the years, his tall frame grew stooped, and his gait shortened, but he kept up a daily walking routine, and Madisonians regularly marked the season with his arrival.

Anyone bold enough to start up a chat with Cooke might have heard stories of government conspiracies to ruin his health. He wasn't bothered much by the authorities, he said, though vandals occasionally slashed a tire or broke a window. He picked up his mail at the post office on Wingra Drive.

Suffering from cancer, he had difficulty breathing last summer, was treated at the veterans hospital, and a few weeks ago entered St. Mary's Care Center, according to Mary Beth Plane, who works near the Arboretum and helped arrange his funeral.

Plane was able to explain one of the mysteries of Cooke's peripatetic wanderings in Madison: What did he do on those long walks every day?

"He planted walnuts," she said. He would pick up walnuts on his walks, and carried a little spade so he could plant them. A bag of walnuts was found in his Winnebago.

He leaves no known survivors.

Beloved Rural Doctor

Dr. Hisham Osman, 1964–2010

MARCH 17, 2010—As a general practitioner serving a rural population, Dr. Hisham Osman's specialty was hearing what his patients didn't say, a quality his friends called "compassionate listening."

These days, nearly three weeks after his death, his circles of influence in the Spring Green area still are being measured.

In Osman, the area Amish had a doctor they could trust, who listened and whose services were affordable.

Patty Ramsden, a nurse, had a boss she stuck with through thick and thin.

Bob Bond had not only a doctor but also a medal-winning badminton partner.

Others had a doctor who would come to their homes to check on their sick children, who would provide medical guidance to the emergency medical service, a hospice program, a nursing home, and two area hospitals.

What they had was a friend, and that was what led them to persuade Osman to turn down a job offer in Minnesota three years ago and start a clinic in Spring Green.

Osman, forty-five, died March 3, about six weeks after feeling ill with abdominal pains, then being surprised with the news he had pancreatic cancer and was going to die soon, leaving a wife and two children.

"It was unbelievably fast. It tore our hearts out," said Ramsden, who had known Osman since he came to Spring Green for a job interview fourteen years ago, fresh off of his residency. "It has been hard for his patients; it's still really hard for them. They can't believe it."

Those patients and other community members were influential in getting Osman, a native of Egypt, to open his unaffiliated clinic in Spring Green three years ago, competing with two other clinics that are part of health care networks.

"He opened the clinic because there were so many things he believed in for patient care," Ramsden said.

Business was a challenge, and like some of his patients, he couldn't afford health insurance. Osman didn't get health insurance until this year.

"Just like opening a business for anybody, it was tough—really, really tough," Ramsden said of challenges such as waiting for insurance payments to arrive.

It will be a challenge to recruit a replacement for Osman, said Phyllis Fritsch, administrator at Upland Hills Health. The Dodgeville-based company, for which Osman had been an on-call doctor, purchased the clinic January 1, just before Osman fell ill.

"He had been an important part of our active medical staff for the past three years, an incredible individual, so personable and quiet. The patients in the community [thought] the world of him," she said. "He would go out of his way to make sure that, whatever situation you were in, that if there was some help he could provide, he would do it, not only for his patients, but to anyone he met."

Bond, president of Cardinal Solar Glass, became Osman's friend first and patient second. He recalled inviting him to his business to meet people when Osman first came to town after leaving the University of Minnesota.

"We just kind of hit it off," he said of Osman, who would become his confidante and his doubles partner in badminton. They built a squash and badminton court in an airplane hangar to work out. "He had the gift of listening—he was a compassionate listener—and hearing what people didn't want to or couldn't say."

Bond said it was common knowledge in the community how costly it was for Osman to run a rural clinic, where he served many patients while trying to keep services affordable. "I think that in opening his own clinic, he really wanted to be a businessman, and he had seen a lot of things in health care where he thought he could offer a service at a lower price and run his own show. It was tough sledding."

That is why the Spring Green community has come together to host a benefit for Osman's family: wife Moshira, daughter Ingie, and son Karim. When Osman died, word spread quickly, but no one really knew what to do, and many had not even been aware he was gravely ill. The benefit, which has been described as a way to give back, is also a way to give thanks.

Familiar Face in Court

Stanley B. Kaufman, 1944–2010

JULY 29, 2010—He was said to be a knowledgeable collector of Cambodian terra-cotta sculptures and Chinese bronze statues.

Unkempt and disheveled, he regularly dozed in corners of the Dane County courthouse, pockets filled with saltines from the cafeteria.

He earned master's and doctorate degrees in philosophy (1982 and 2002) and a law degree (1984) from the University of Wisconsin–Madison.

It was a standing joke that if there was free food anywhere in the courthouse, that's where you would find him.

Stanley B. Kaufman, sixty-five, longtime Madison lawyer, philosopher, and antique art collector, died July 10 in a New York City hotel, of what authorities called natural causes. His death caused nary a ripple in the legal tides of Madison because, the consummate loner, there was no one here to contact about his death. He has a brother in upstate New York, acquaintances said, and an aunt who lives in Miami.

Kaufman was a one-man law firm. His meal tickets came from public defender assignments for the most routine of criminal cases, and he was considered adept at bankruptcy cases.

Kaufman's law office was in his condo of 828 square feet, one of four living units in the historic Braley House at 422 North Henry

Street, walking distance to the courthouse. Arthur Braley was a famous Wisconsin judge and Shakespearean scholar in the 1880s.

At the New York City Manhattan Office of the Chief Medical Examiner, public affairs director Ellen Borakove said Monday the cause of Kaufman's death was not determined and that the body had not been claimed. A New York City police detective said Kaufman died of natural causes.

"Shy but interesting," said Katherine Dorl, at the Dane County Public Defender's Office, of Kaufman. "Everyone has their Stan Kaufman story, and everyone seemed to know a different part of him. There wasn't a lot of pizzazz. He just quietly did his work."

Fellow defense attorneys called him "a demented genius," "a guy with a voracious appetite," "one strange cat." Kaufman also wrote letters to the editor on topics affecting downtown Madison, where he lived. He defended the homeless, arguing they were blamed for more ills than they caused. He also wanted more enforcement scrutiny aimed at "young hooligans who are predominantly middle class" rather than street alcoholics.

"He performed better than he looked, which was always kind of rough. I never saw him in a jacket, and if there was a tie, it was askew," said Dane County Circuit Court Judge William Foust, who first met Kaufman when the two were philosophy students at UW–Madison. "Intellectually he was probably head and shoulders above most of the people he ever dealt with, but when it came to street smarts and common sense, then he was in the back of the line."

According to the State Bar of Wisconsin, earlier this year Kaufman received the Harry & Velma Hamilton Branch Service Award from the Madison branch of the NAACP for "his steadfast and exemplary volunteer efforts." Mike Verveer, as alderman in Kaufman's district, knew him as well as anyone. Verveer said he was a prickly constituent and familiar figure on State Street, where he could be found sitting in the corner of Qdoba Mexican Grill, reading a newspaper and avoiding eye contact.

"He clearly was a night owl," Verveer said.

Gretchen and Benjamin Atkinson, who live in one of the four condos as neighbors across the hall to Kaufman, described Kaufman as "very opinionated" and busier than ever with bankruptcy cases.

But he made time for interests beyond the law. "He was very much interested in African masks and artifacts and would go to New York City to meet with antique dealers and collectors," she said.

He was on his annual trip to New York when he died.

Kaufman also was active in the politics and preservation efforts of the Mansion Hill neighborhood, where he lived, and with the Capital Neighborhood Association. "He was interested in getting this house restored to its former grandeur," Atkinson said.

The house on North Henry Street was designated a landmark in 1976. According to the Federal Writers' Project guide to Wisconsin, the Braley Home was once occupied by writer-poet and reincarnation fantasist Ella Wheeler Wilcox, who while living there wrote the immortal lines from "Solitude": "Laugh, and the world laughs with you; Weep, and you weep alone."

Circus Owner and More

Bill Griffith, 1929–2010

OCTOBER 12, 2010—A true account of Bill Griffith's life could have filled all three rings of the circuses he owned and the front pages of all the newspapers he published.

Griffith, who died Sunday at eighty-one, wrote his own obituary and achieved the impossible by underselling himself.

"We were trying to list all the businesses he owned or started, and we're still at it," said daughter Linda Schwanke, co-owner of the Spring Green weekly, the *Home News*.

Not to exaggerate, but Griffith played trumpet in his own polka band, bought and sold and bought again nearly two dozen little Wisconsin newspapers and shoppers, personally promoted the Harmonicats and the Ink Spots, and was the owner or part owner of a trio of three-ring circuses that were based in Appleton and traveled to thirty-four states.

He did not shy from describing things as the best, the first, the largest, and he really was the last—he claimed—surviving three-ring circus owner in Wisconsin.

Not surprisingly, he loved the opera and treasured a large photograph of his first elephant, Little Bertha.

He smoked big cigars and accumulated a stupendous collection of antique circus air calliopes and put them on display until, he noted in his obit, he "found out that most of today's families never

Bill Griffith at the American Calliope Center, which he opened in Spring
Green in 1998 to display his collection of circus calliopes.
CRAIG SCHREINER, *WISCONSIN STATE JOURNAL*

heard of calliopes." Schwanke said her father, an Appleton native
and printer by trade, was not an idle worshipper.

"He grew up in the Depression. His motivation was he just
had to hustle a buck. He always had to have some business going,"
she said. "He didn't have hobbies."

But it was the circus that guided his life. He was always looking
for a promotion, a flair, or a new way to package an old favorite, such
as having Santa Claus arrive in a spaceship at shopping centers.

"When he was an itty bitty boy, he went to the Ringling circus
when it came to Appleton," Schwanke said. "He didn't run away
to one. He started his own. He wasn't a circus fan. He was a circus
person. He lived for circuses."

Griffith requested calliope music and a Frank Sinatra rendi-
tion of "I Did It My Way" for his funeral. The services will take
place at 4 p.m. Thursday at Richardson-Stafford Funeral Home
in Spring Green.

Holocaust Survivor

Erwin Deutsch, 1916–2010

DECEMBER 7, 2010—When Erwin Deutsch got out of Buchenwald in 1938, he vowed to his new wife, Steffi, that he would never forget, but he wouldn't let the experience of following his father to a concentration camp haunt him.

Instead, his experiences haunt others, and many people who had "never met a Jew" gave tearful embraces to a modest man dedicated to interpreting one of the great evils of the twentieth century.

Deutsch, who had lived in Madison since 1997 and spoke frequently to groups about the Holocaust, died Saturday at ninety-four. "Life had dealt him a lot of challenges, which he met," said his daughter, Renata Bennett, of Madison. "He wasn't a jolly man. He was pretty serious, but he wasn't a sad man either. He made the best of his life, and he was incredibly generous with himself and his time."

Deutsch started talking publicly about the Holocaust and its causes after he turned eighty, when a chance conversation led to Deutsch's first talk to a high school class.

"When I was done, the students came up to me and put their arms around me and were hugging me with tears running down their faces," he said. "I decided that whenever I am asked, I am going to talk."

What he talked about was his time at Buchenwald, a Nazi concentration camp near Weimar, Germany. He entered the camp on November 10, 1938, the day following Kristallnacht, the night the

Nazis began a massive pogrom against Jewish families. Nazis arrested
Deutsch's father in Breslau, Germany, and took him to the camps.

Deutsch, who was twenty-two years
old at the time, turned himself in the
next day so he could find and rescue
his father. He was at Buchenwald
nearly a month before being released
with his father on the promise they
would leave the country by the end
of December.

What followed was a frantic and
dangerous journey. The family left
from Hamburg on January 9, 1939—
Deutsch was a fanatic about dates

Erwin Deutsch.
CRAIG SCHREINER, *WISCONSIN
STATE JOURNAL*

and could remember details from every journey—with the
equivalent of four dollars and one suitcase per person.

As he explained in an interview in 2004, their journey included
phony names entered at a home for the elderly, transport arranged
and canceled, bribes, lies, tricks, and broken promises. They per-
severed with what Deutsch proudly described as "chutzpah," an
audacity fueled by fear and self-preservation.

Deutsch eventually brought his family in 1946 to St. Louis, where
he worked as a bricklayer, before moving in 1958 to New Orleans,
where he began a small successful construction company.

Deutsch was most often invited to speak during Holocaust
Remembrance Week. One of his frequent topics was Nazi law, the
framework of injustice that led step by step to the Final Solution,
the planned genocide of Jews during World War II.

"I'll never forget it, but I won't let it haunt me. If I get one
person who listens to me who will not forget it either, then it was
worth the time to talk about it."

A funeral for Erwin Deutsch will be held at 11 a.m. Wednesday
at Cress Funeral Home, 3610 Speedway Road, Madison.

Squash Man

Lennie Huebner, 1943–2011

MARCH 3, 2011—Lennie Huebner would bring his partner David Wescom on foraging trips in the fall. They drove their little white car right into Don Schuster's farm fields outside Deerfield and stuffed that car so full of squash its rear dragged all the way to the nearest food pantry.

They would return for a refill and hit the next pantry, in Deerfield, Sun Prairie, the AIDS Support Network, wherever anyone needed free food.

It was usually acorn squash, destined to be plowed under as fertilizer because there is a heap of bother and no profit in harvesting the surplus for sale.

"Lennie has been coming here forever," said Schuster. "I've seen those guys fill up that car ten times in a day."

Leonard Huebner, known to many as Lennie or simply "the squash man," died of cancer February 21. He was the oldest of eleven children in a family that immigrated to Wisconsin from New Zealand, where he was born.

Frugal but generous, he could not bear to see anything go to waste nor any need unfilled, said Michael Hansen, a friend who also was Huebner's caregiver for the past few months.

If you mentioned in passing that you enjoyed a certain recipe, there was good chance Huebner would leave a casserole on your porch the next day. Sidewalks were shoveled, flowers delivered (he was an orchid grower), pies and pumpkin cheesecakes baked, all from his and Wescom's trailer home in Marshall.

After retiring from Oscar Mayer, he worked at part-time jobs such as cleaning Sun Prairie's City Hall. There he got to know Diane Hermann-Brown, the city clerk, who often works late.

"Leonard was a sweetheart, the first in line to give to other people," Hermann-Brown said, recalling the way the counters at City Hall bloomed when Huebner's daffodils and other flowers were in season. "He wasn't just the squash man. He was the flower man, too, the green man."

Hansen said Huebner, who was diagnosed HIV positive twenty-one years ago, had many other health issues. That gave him the advantage of perspective and context, said Hermann-Brown.

"He didn't have a lot in life, but what he had, he shared," she said.

D-Day Survivor

Jack O'Donnell, 1922–2011

NOVEMBER 10, 2011—Jack O'Donnell, who died Tuesday at age eighty-nine, wondered at surviving the Normandy Invasion while all around him young men died.

It was June 1944, and he was in Company L, Eighteenth Infantry Regiment, First Infantry Division, and he was in the first group of assault troops to hit Omaha Beach.

For the fiftieth anniversary of D-Day in 1994, he wrote about his experience for the *Capital Times*: "That's the way it was at Omaha. It was a rite of passage for those who survived that bloody day. And I wondered at being spared. There were fathers being taken from their wives and children. Were they not better men than I?"

Francis "Jack" O'Donnell lied to get into the National Guard at the age of fifteen, joined the army in 1940, fought through the bloodiest of campaigns in World War II, and was known for his gentle nature.

Like many World War II veterans' obituaries, the fine print of O'Donnell's reveals little detail of astonishing sacrifices and no acclaim, commensurate with a quiet desire to avoid it.

O'Donnell left the army in 1962 with a chest full of medals he did not show off or relish discussing. They included a Purple Heart with three clusters, meaning four times wounded in combat, nearly

Jack O'Donnell. DAVID SANDELL,
CAPITAL TIMES

mortally in North Africa. He also was awarded the Bronze Star with cluster and the Distinguished Service Cross, the nation's second-highest combat award, for "extraordinary heroism." An article in the *Fort Sheridan Tower* in 1951 noted he was the most decorated soldier at the Illinois base. He earned the award by killing nine enemy soldiers with his rifle and grenades as he and his squad withdrew during a German counterattack on June 10, 1944.

His son Jim said he endured back operations and poor vision for the rest of his life from injuries suffered in infantry campaigns and battles in Africa, Sicily, Normandy, and on into Germany. He stayed in after the war and was sent to Japan and Korea.

He and wife, Rita, raised six children—all born in different states—on Commonwealth Avenue in Madison.

"He was a soft-spoken guy, a great dad," Jim O'Donnell said. "He didn't talk about his time in the war a lot. He always said he was no hero. He said the heroes were the ones who didn't make it back. I think of him as my hero."

Jim said Wednesday that his dad was a library assistant at the Madison Public Library, working in the card catalogues. In his obituary, his family said Jack O'Donnell enjoyed writing poetry and considered sharing important. He liked baseball and a good joke. Apple pie and ice cream "brought him comfort on good days and bad."

A private service will be held on Friday, Veterans Day.

A Pioneer of Affordable Legal Help

Ken Hur, 1924–2012

JANUARY 4, 2012—Ken Hur, the effervescent, wavy-haired lawyer who introduced legal advertising to Madison airwaves and enjoyed poking the vested tummies of his staid barrister brethren, died December 30 at the Wisconsin Veterans Home at King.

"My whole life has been a series of anecdotes," he liked to say, and he never tired of relating or adding to them.

Impishly louche and quotable, Hur ran the Legal Clinic in Madison, pioneering cheap legal help and sloganeering: "Talk to a lawyer for just ten bucks." In his most famous television commercial, the manatee-shaped Hur—born Hurwitz in Syracuse, New York, in 1924—emerged wearing beads, long necklaces, and scuba gear from a swimming pool, telling potential bankruptcy customers: "If you're in over your head, we'll put you through bankruptcy for only one hundred dollars."

"Advertising was a natural for him," Hur's daughter Tamara Sue Kaplan said. "He was an actor. All his life he was just trying to bring affordable legal help to people. He didn't think the people should be intimidated by the law."

He had an airplane fly over Badgers football games pulling his name on a banner. He had a parked crunched car with the message painted on it "Sideswiped? Call Ken Hur."

"People should not be afraid to go in to see a lawyer with a

Ken Hur. L. ROGER TURNER, *WISCONSIN STATE JOURNAL*

fresh crisp ten dollar bill and say: 'Here, lawyer, talk this much,'"
Hur told the *Wisconsin State Journal* in 1977, when he ran his first
television ads and was expecting disapproval from the Wisconsin
Bar Association.

Hur came to Madison and Truax Field at the age of seventeen
and then returned after World War II. He attended the University
of Wisconsin and lived in Badger Village with wife, Jacquie, outside
of Baraboo, where he was justice of the peace. His constable in the
village, a housing complex across from the Badger Army Ammunition
Plant, was Lee Dreyfus, who later became governor.

When his income dropped, he would dispatch Lee to "go out
and nail a few speeders because I'd get to keep the two dollar court
costs," recalled Hur.

Hur faced various legal problems himself, including bankruptcy, through the years but never shied from the spotlight.

Hur recently returned to Wisconsin after spending most of
his retirement in Key Largo, Florida. He was eighty-seven and is
survived by five children. His wife died in 2004.

Great Ape

Casey, c. 1982–2013

MARCH 7, 2013—Casey, thirty-one, a chimpanzee raised in Rockford, Illinois, by a gorilla wrestler and a doted-upon resident of the Vilas Zoo since 1995, died Wednesday from an unknown cause after a physical examination, Dane County officials reported.

Zoo staff was described as "shocked and saddened" at the death. The physical was supposed to be routine, said Carrie Springer of the Dane County Executive Office, adding that Casey was middle-aged for a chimpanzee. The death leaves the zoo with two adult chimpanzees: Cookie and Magadi.

Casey, who was reportedly able to ride a rocking horse, play football, and drink from a bottle at the age of one month, was one of twenty-six chimps raised by Milton and Winona Kling, who trained animals and ran an amusement park.

Casey died during anesthetic recovery, following the physical exam and "diagnostic procedures," according to Springer. The tests, a collaboration between the zoo staff and the UW School of Veterinary Medicine, included blood collection, cardiac ultrasound, and X-rays.

"Casey was a well-loved animal and a favorite of many at our zoo. He will be dearly missed by zoo staff and the community," said Ronda Schwetz, director of the Vilas Zoo.

Zoo officials said a postmortem process, part of the Association of Zoos and Aquariums Chimpanzee Species Survival Plan, will be

Casey the chimpanzee, pictured at Henry Vilas Zoo. DANE COUNTY EXECUTIVE'S OFFICE

used to determine the cause of death. The data will also be contributed to the Great Ape Heart Project, which addresses cardiovascular disease, a common occurrence in great apes.

Casey's history in Madison, according to newspaper archives, dates to 1995, the year the zoo's primate house opened. Casey joined Cookie as donations from the Klings, who had raised the chimps—and many others—in their Rockford home. Their arrival at the zoo was unusual in that they had not been raised in another zoo.

A newspaper article from the time noted that when the chimps first saw the Klings after they were donated to the zoo, the chimps "were so hurt they wouldn't even wave back . . . they turned their backs on them instead, in a kind of protest."

Groundbreaking Immunogeneticist

Jan Rapacz, 1928–2013

MAY 8, 2013—Jan Rapacz, eighty-four, a brilliant and persistent immunogeneticist whose mutant pigs became a standard in heart disease research, died Sunday in Krakow, in his native Poland.

Rapacz, who also conducted groundbreaking work with mink early in his Madison career, was a ski jumper, orchid grower, and pioneer in developing a pig the perfect size and quality for research: a small pig that dies young of high cholesterol levels and clogged arteries. It is called the "Rapacz familial hypercholesterolemic pig," or the RFH pig.

Rapacz worked for decades with his research partner and wife, Judith Hasler-Rapacz. At first with little attention or funding, he would store pig hearts for as long as eight years waiting for analysis. He was at the University of Wisconsin–Madison from 1971 to 2004. He first came here, though, in 1961, to conduct studies on mink infertility, after which he returned to Poland to start a program to test parentage in cattle.

Rapacz said his research would never have gotten off the ground without the aid of herdsmen at the university's Arlington Farms, where the pig strain was developed. It was also the scene of perhaps the professor's greatest sadness, as a fire in December 1995 killed nearly the entire population. Four surviving pigs were found in the fire rubble days after the fire, and the unique strain continued.

Jan Rapacz, pictured in 1987, studied heart-diseased pigs such as this one.
MICHAEL KIENITZ

Millard Susman, retired genetics department chairman, said Rapacz joined the University of Wisconsin and a group of researchers at a time when "immunogenetics was very hot stuff, and the pioneers were here."

Rapacz was "enormously enthusiastic and energetic, he lived a life full of joy and energy," he said.

"He sure had a lot of energy. He could be so energized it would be difficult to understand what he was saying," agreed Dan Schaefer, chairman at the Department of Animal Science. He said biomedical use of the Rapacz pig—a "durable discovery"—continues.

Rapacz's discoveries and adventures with pigs were included in the book *Altered Fates: Gene Therapy and the Retooling of Human Life* by Jeff Lyon and Peter Gorner. In it, Rapacz recalled that when World War II ended in 1945, after spending five years in the forest with his family because of the Nazi occupation, he was fifteen years old and could neither read nor write. "My teachers told my dad to take me back to the farm and let me be a shepherd," he said.

Instead, he "studied like a demon," the book said. He earned his BS, MS, and PhD from the University of Jagiellonica in Krakow.

Rapacz is survived by his wife, two children, and four grandchildren.

Helped but Not Saved

David Luettgen, 1982–2013

MAY 11, 2013—Friday was going to be a big day for thirty-year-old David Luettgen in Madison.

Blind, homeless, and recovering from surgery, he had been adopted by a group of volunteers who, in fewer than forty-eight hours, had set up a plan to get him a place to stay, a case manager, a mobile phone, even a new cane to help him get around. They didn't tuck him in Thursday night at his homeless shelter bunk, but they made sure he got there safely.

Friday morning, he didn't wake up.

Luettgen's cause of death was not immediately determined, reported the Dane County Medical Examiner's Office, where an autopsy was conducted Friday morning. The office could not confirm his identity either, but friends told the *State Journal* he was known as "Blind Dave" and used the last names of Luettgen and Nauer.

Tami Miller, an advocate for the poor and homeless, mustered like-minded helpers Wednesday and Thursday to come to the aid of the disabled man, who lost both eyes to glaucoma several years ago, she said.

"When I spoke to him last night, he was so happy that he had a case manager and a place to stay, and we were getting him a phone and a new cane. He was so grateful for the help," Miller said via a Facebook page, "Feeding the State Street Family."

"For the most part, the system worked pretty well as soon as he reached out to ask for help. I was so afraid of him sleeping outside by himself. He was such a vulnerable person," she said. "This morning, he didn't show up for his ride, and the rumors were out there about a blind man dying."

Police were called at 5:48 a.m. to a Porchlight-managed shelter called Shelter Two to check on an unresponsive man. The shelter holds fifty men.

Debbie Magnusen, a longtime Madison friend who was part of the group who assisted him, struggled Friday with the shock, and said Luettgen had a difficult life in the past few years.

"He had a lot of issues in his life. Being blind was only one of them," she said. "He was a sociable guy, liked to joke, and didn't like to be alone, but sometimes people took advantage of him being blind."

In addition, he had been ill recently and had surgery in Janesville last week, she said: "Everybody here was busting themselves trying to get him help."

"I am so saddened that he was not able to make it through and realize that he was not all alone in the world, that people do care," Miller said. "Life didn't have to be this hard for him."

One of the Greatest Generation

Eugene P. Moran, 1924–2014

MARCH 27, 2014—Eugene P. Moran, eighty-nine, who survived a ride on the shot-up tail section of a falling Flying Fortress bomber in 1943, then endured eighteen months as a prisoner of war, died Sunday in Soldiers Grove.

Moran's motto was, "I'd rather wear out than rust out," according to his obituary in the *State Journal* Wednesday.

A Crawford County native, Moran enlisted in the US Army Air Corps in October 1942. A year later, he was the tail gunner in a B-17 Flying Fortress, on his fifth bombing mission, flying near Bremen, when the plane encountered heavy fire.

According to the narrative in a Veterans Lifetime Achievement Award he received in 2007: "With severe gunshot wounds and a bullet-riddled parachute, he rode the tail section down at the rate of 100 feet per second; and he survived the descent, but sustained a crushed skull when the tail section hit a tree trunk before crashing to the ground; his life was saved by a Serbian doctor, also a POW, who surgically repaired his severe head wounds after which he was a prisoner of war for almost eighteen months, inhumanely incarcerated in POW camps in Germany, Prussia, and Poland, and surviving solitary confinement, relocation on a 'hell ship' on the Baltic Sea, and a six-hundred-mile forced march from early February to late April 1945 during one of the harshest winters on record."

Liberated on April 26, 1945, at Bitterfelt, Germany, Moran was discharged December 1, awarded two Purple Hearts, the Air Medal with Gold Leaf Cluster, and other medals. He weighed 128 pounds when liberated.

In the next year, he would marry Margaret "Peg" Finley and move to Soldiers Grove, where they raised nine children.

According to his obituary, he was a rural mail carrier for more than thirty years, a volunteer firefighter, chaired numerous service projects, and was a charter member of the rescue squad and a twenty-year member of the Crawford County Board. In 2008, the village dedicated a street in the village park in his honor.

In a 2007 interview for the federal Veterans History Project, Moran recalled why he enlisted: "Well, when I was kid there on the farm, on a nice bright day I would be lying there and looking up at the sky and see those planes, and I always said someday I'll be in one of them, and I did."

In that same interview, Moran described the forced march of prisoners at the end of the war: "Well, we started marching February the eighth and we marched until, I think it was the seventeenth of April we got liberated. I figure about six trips from Soldiers Grove to Minneapolis."

One Half of a Donkey Duo

Mo, c. 1996–2014

MAY 5, 2014—The painted plywood heads of donkeys named Mo and Jo have identified the hoofed inhabitants of the paddock at the corner of Highways CC and D seven miles south of Madison for eighteen years.

Last week, a black bag was placed over the "Mo" sign, and the spot started attracting bright-colored memorials.

Mo died April 25, and Jo has been braying his loneliness ever since.

The Sicilian miniature donkeys, who were not related, were purchased eighteen years ago by Keith and Merrlyn Schoville. The donkeys were living landmarks at the intersection, "known all over the world," Merrlyn said. This type of donkey is often described as "tame, affectionate, gentle, and friendly," and these two were all of that.

Mo died of complications from laminitis, which he got from overeating during the long winter. "He's the pig of the two," and ate too heartily, she said. He was under a veterinarian's care and had been showing signs of improvement, so the death was hard for the Schovilles to take.

None took it harder than his companion, Jo.

"Jo is totally lost without Mo. He cries all the time, or just stands in the shed and cries," she said, explaining it was really more

Jo the donkey grazes in the background of an impromptu memorial for Mo at the donkeys' home in the town of Oregon. AMBER ARNOLD, *WISCONSIN STATE JOURNAL*

like a constant bray. "It is so sad. He is used to playing with Mo. They chased each other and played."

A new companion for Jo, an eleven-month-old male from a donkey rescue outfit whose name will be Jack, arrived on Sunday.

"We just released him into the area with Joseph, and they're getting acquainted as donkeys do," Keith said Sunday afternoon.

Jo wasn't letting the curious Jack get too close, responding with a mild warning kick when his personal space was violated.

"They're out there enjoying the beautiful day. We don't expect we'll have any problems with them getting along," Keith said.

Final Dispatch

John Ottinger, 1937–2014

JULY 3, 2014—John Ottinger, seventy-six, an expert on Madison street homonyms, organizer of a self-acclaimed accordion marching band, cab driver, and the calming voice of the Madison overnight police dispatch from 1978 through the nineties, died Tuesday of chronic lung disease caused by smoking.

Ottinger was a lover of words, especially puns, and of precision, especially in giving directions. He was, then, a perfect dispatcher, who knew Milton Street was not accessible off West Washington Avenue, though a contemporary street directory said it was. He knew Sheridan Street and Sheridan Drive are a half-mile apart and have duplicate house numbers. He knew East Washington Avenue used to be called Sun Prairie Road, a valuable bit of information if a street directory said Algoma Street was just off it.

He bit his tongue over Greenway Cross, Greenway Road, and Greenway Trail and the fifteen or so "Lake something-or-others" in Madison, including a Lakeview Avenue and a Lake View Avenue. His favorite Madison street, he noted in a 1984 interview, was Wayne Street, south of Milwaukee Street, off Leon on the East Side, just big enough for one house.

Before Dane County switched on its 911 system in 1989, police dispatchers talked with emergency callers and directed police to where they were needed.

"He was very calming" to both officers and callers, said Peggy Lison, Ottinger's wife. "The worst things could be going on out there, and if you heard his voice, you felt better. His attitude to the cops on the street was that he had their backs."

Lison said her husband's best stories were unprintable, then shared a couple that were: taking pizza orders from wrong-number callers, for example.

His 1984 Police Department Street Directory was of great appeal to cops, cab drivers, garage sale hunters, delivery people, and late-shift newspaper reporters. The latter might have been favored occasionally by the gruff Ottinger, who at eighteen found work in California as a copy boy for the *Los Angeles Times* and who carried pencil and notebook as a police reporter in Rockford, Illinois, before moving to Madison in the 1960s.

When he retired from the police department in 1998, his calm under pressure, nose for detail, and dry sense of humor were dispatching legends. He also had amazing recall of the habits of frequent callers to the police department, a timely talent that mitigated the surprise a rookie cop might meet in responding to Madison's eccentric populace.

He knew that there was a greenhouse behind the white house, or that the one house usually had red geraniums on the porch.

A dedicated birder and canoeist, Ottinger went public as an accordion player when he helped organize the Sesqueezecentennial Accordion Marching Band, an amateur group formed at no public expense to help celebrate the state's 150th birthday in 1998 and beyond.

When the first edition of his Madison Police Department Street Directory came out, its two hundred copies sold out immediately. That was fine with the meticulous Ottinger, who found a couple of mistakes to correct in the next printing.

The most notable was at the end of the book, where every school, park, and church was supposed to be listed with address.

He inadvertently left out all of the Presbyterian churches, and admitted, "I was getting punchy...so I guess I wasn't paying attention at the end there."

That would have been the first time.

The Mayor of the Mazomanie Nude Beach

Charlie Wise, 1952–2015

December 11, 2015—A male body was found Thursday afternoon along the Wisconsin River near where longtime resident Charlie H. Wise, who was once the unofficial "mayor" and de facto caretaker of the Mazomanie nude beach, parked his car and went missing three days ago.

The Dane County Sheriff's Office set up an extended search Thursday on Department of Natural Resources property, hoping to find Wise, sixty-three. Sheriff's officials said Wise had been living in his purple Mercury Mystique, which was found Friday parked along Highway Y in the town of Mazomanie, in an area known as the Mazomanie Oak Barrens.

According to Dane County Sheriff's Lieutenant Dave Dohnal, a body was found at 2:27 p.m. in a wooded area about one-third of a mile from where Wise's car was parked. Friday, the body was identified as Wise. The Dane County Medical Examiner's Office ruled the death a suicide.

Wise had been living at an assisted-living apartment in Sauk City but was evicted in late November.

A former lawyer, Wise was originally from the Twin Cities area and came to Mazomanie to live at the Wisconsin River's nude beach area in 1996, as reported in a 2007 profile of Wise published in the *Wisconsin State Journal*. When he arrived at the nude beach

Charlie Wise, pictured in 2007. CRAIG SCHREINER, *WISCONSIN STATE JOURNAL*

in 1996, he set up housekeeping in his 1989 Dodge van, to the
consternation of DNR wardens.

His exit from Minnesota followed the dissolution of his second
marriage and a dive into a deep depression that left him on
disability, he said in 2007. He decided the best treatment would
be administered from a spot on a beach along the Wisconsin River,
where he lived in his van and tents until 2008.

"I guess I am at the end of my rope," he said then. He was a lanky
six foot two, his teeth were falling out, and he was covered in scabs
from a longstanding skin infection.

He had a prescription for his depression, and occasionally friends
would spot him some cash, but he was living on a small monthly
disability check, most of which he said went to pay child support.

In November 2007, cold, broke, depressed, jobless, mentally
and physically ill, in debt, and living in a van with a broken heater

next to a nude beach, he put on an old pinstriped suit and a pair of black wingtips and drove to Madison to, as he put it, "sell myself."

He talked with a reporter because he figured it was either that or freeze to death. "I'm in a spot where my vehicle gets ten miles to the gallon. The blower in my heater went out. Not a big deal to most people, but it is virtually life and death to me."

He had, however, taken to attending the New Heights Lutheran Parish, which has churches in Mazomanie and Black Earth. With help from the local pastor completing paperwork, Wise was hoping his financial situation might improve.

The living situation did. A Black Earth landlord read the newspaper story and found Wise a free unfurnished apartment for the winter. A local dental clinic stepped forward with emergency care and a plan for long-term repairs.

For the past four years, he had reportedly been living in assisted-living apartments in the Sauk Prairie area.

He said in 2007 he had been making a video journal of his time on the river and hoped to turn it into a program about his life.

Wise had been in and out of trouble with the DNR and other law enforcement agencies over the past nineteen years, mostly for trespassing but also for possession of marijuana and lewd and lascivious conduct.

Life after Presumed Death

Donald Heiliger, 1937–2016

MARCH 27, 2016—Donald Heiliger, seventy-nine, died Wednesday, more than forty years after assumptions of his death in the Vietnam War turned out to be false.

The Madison native and Air Force pilot was a prisoner of war in Vietnam from May 15, 1967, to February 18, 1973, enduring brutal torture, beatings, and privation. His parents did not know he was alive until November 1969, and he was not listed publicly as a prisoner until April 1970.

After returning to Madison, the Air Force major remained in the service for a time, worked for the government, then became a real estate agent and a bus driver. He was elected to the Dane County Board in 1992 and served six terms as a conservative member representing the Stoughton area.

His capture was by parts harrowing and lucky: Heiliger, on his second tour of duty in Vietnam, was a captain and one of two crew members on an F-105 flying a low-level bombing run thirty miles northeast of Hanoi.

"Five seconds before bombs away we were hit. . . . I don't know if it was a shot or a rocket. We tried to put out the fire without much luck," he described in an interview with the *Wisconsin State Journal* in April 1973, when he first talked about being tortured.

Donald Heiliger in 1997 with a model of an F-105 jet similar to the one he flew in Vietnam. JOSEPH W. JACKSON III, *WISCONSIN STATE JOURNAL*

They had to increase altitude just to be able to bail out, after which he floated in his parachute for "about ten minutes," then landed, suffering only minor injuries. He hid from villages for several hours before being caught, while munching on a chocolate bar. The other crew member, Major Ben Pollard, was also captured and later returned.

That was the start of Heiliger's long captivity in four prisons in North Vietnam, where he was tortured under interrogation. Screw cuffs were attached to his wrists, and his ankles were attached with U-shaped irons to an eight-foot steel bar.

Besides the torture, he endured frequent beatings by guards, he said. Treatment improved in fall 1969, after the death of Ho Chi Minh, he said. His parents first heard he was alive in August of that year. At that point, he was allowed to send letters twice a year to his parents, limited to six lines. Before that, he said, "My dad was convinced I was dead."

While he was held prisoner, his wife divorced him and remarried, moving to Ohio with their three children. He was released with other prisoners as part of a series of "goodwill gesture" releases following a January 27, 1973, ceasefire that promised prisoner releases within sixty days. The resulting wave of arrivals back in the United States was an emotional roller coaster for the families and the entire country. It was not until the release of the final prisoners that Heiliger talked about the torture.

Heiliger's return to Madison came on March 9, 1973, when he was met by a crowd of three hundred people at Four Lakes Aviation on Highway 51.

"It's great to be back home. I can't help but feel great being back in Madison," he said, as the mayor gave him a key to the city and a host of children waved American flags. At a news conference that day, he said, though he had no bitterness toward those who were in the anti-war movement, he believed those actions prolonged the war, a sentiment he repeated in interviews.

Heiliger jumped right into an active life, returning to school. In December 1973, he married Cheryl Kay Edwards, a graduate student in speech therapy. Four of his ex-POW comrades attended.

Heiliger was a University of Wisconsin–Madison graduate in accounting, had joined the air force in 1958, and was flying jets solo in 1964.

On the county board, Heiliger was a staunch, reliable conservative, former board colleague Dave Wiganowsky said.

"He didn't talk much about his stay in the prison camps," Wiganowsky said. "He was a laid-back guy who would think before he talked, a very intelligent man."

Dennis O'Loughlin, another board colleague, who served twenty-five years in the Air National Guard, found a kindred soul and valued adviser in Heiliger: "Don was a realist. He was conservative but in his performance on the board he was fair. If you can say that about anybody, that is a good thing."

Revered and Feared Math Teacher

Sherry Masters, 1946–2016

NOVEMBER 10, 2016—Sherry Masters, seventy, died November 3, three weeks after being diagnosed with leukemia. She taught mathematics and manners to people who hated math, and she enjoyed strolling with her appropriately outfitted toy poodle, Chauncey.

Before he died last year, Chauncey sat on her lap when she drove her car, occasionally honking the horn at stoplights. Masters also dressed him in people clothes and pushed him around the Hilldale Shopping Center area in a stroller, occasionally asking passersby if they didn't think her son looked like a dog.

She had a sense for finding the humor in life and once was a fencing instructor at a camp that had no fencing equipment, so she had to use golf clubs.

Masters retired from Madison Area Technical College in 2004 after thirty-five years of teaching mathematics, mostly to "math-phobic" students, according to her obituary.

She was "a revered and feared mathematics instructor ... having successfully taught thousands of math-phobic students to come to class on time, show their work, and stop talking among themselves."

She liked Johnny Cash and Woody Allen movies and hated the phrases "mission statements" and "strategic initiatives."

Sherry Masters with her toy poodle Chauncey in 2005. JOSEPH W. JACKSON III, *WISCONSIN STATE JOURNAL*

But she loved her teaching job, she told the *State Journal* in 2005: "Ever since I was three years old I wanted to be a teacher. When I was in high school I had the most wonderful math teacher. All I wanted to do was follow in his footsteps. I felt I accomplished this when a student here in Madison told me I reminded him of his high school teacher back in New York. It turns out his teacher was this same man who was such an inspiration to me."

There will be no funeral. Donations were suggested to the OccuPaws Guide Dog Association or the Jewish Federation of Madison.

Norwegian Myth Buster

Harald S. Naess, 1925–2017

FEBRUARY 10, 2017—Harald S. Naess, an affable, accessible professor who for many years was Wisconsin's go-to guy for answers to all questions about Norway, died Sunday in Kristiansand, Norway, where he grew up. He was ninety-one.

A polite and engaged storyteller, Naess taught from 1959 to 1991 in the University of Wisconsin–Madison Department of Scandinavian Studies, the first in the United States. He was chairman for several years in the 1960s, during the department's greatest expansion.

His specialty was Norwegian author and Nobel Prize winner Knut Hamsun—who in his youth lived a penurious existence in Elroy, Wisconsin—but he taught many courses over his thirty-plus years in the department. He also delighted in answering questions about Norwegian culture and myths, especially in a state where those myths die hard and where many residents claim a status as descendants from Scandinavian immigrants.

Asked in 1989 about lutefisk and lefse suppers, which are still popular in Wisconsin churches, Naess said, first of all, in Norway the people don't socialize in churches, few of which have the basements that usually host those activities here. And second, "Norwegians have electric freezers today. They don't need to have dried cod."

Norwegians aren't big on hugs, either, he added: "Norwegians don't touch. This embracing? All this 'Have a nice day'? It is unknown to Norwegians."

Naess himself was far from taciturn. His was a welcoming figure, constantly traveling the state to talk about Norway, Norwegians, and the immigrant experience, often with a summer school course that visited Wisconsin's Norwegian settlements.

Harald Naess. *WISCONSIN STATE JOURNAL*

Early days earning his living teaching could be rough. Once, while teaching in the 1960s at the University of Minnesota, which rotated hosting summer school courses with UW, one of the students "wondered why I always wore the same tie. He did not know that we lived, wife, husband, and three kids, in a tent in a Minnesota park."

Their permanent home for many years was a farm in the town of Springdale, outside of Mount Horeb, that they called Maridal. The couple moved back to Norway in the mid-1990s.

"He loved to build things, out on that farm and in the department, too," said Kim Nilsson, a longtime colleague and also a retired Scandinavian studies professor. Another colleague, Richard Vowles, wrote of a "peculiarly Naessian ritual," which was to host a secret fish boil at Picnic Point on Christmas Eve. Vowles described Naess's "essence" as equal parts accessibility, modesty, and geniality with "the ability to translate life's indignities into a comic scenario."

Naess kept his research going long after retirement, editing six volumes of Hamsun's letters and a 350-page explanation of Latin and Greek plant names.

Acknowledgments

Fred Curran was the night city editor at the *Wisconsin State Journal* in May 1972, when I sat down at the obit desk behind a Remington typewriter, inserted two sheets of copy paper separated by carbon paper, and started writing about dead people. Thank you, Fred, for making me care.

Later editors let me write what I wanted, and I thank them, too. They were Frank Denton, who took the phone calls and the grief; Cliff Behnke, who demanded clean copy and who encouraged shaking things up; Joyce Dehli, who quietly encouraged it; and Brian Howell, who made sure it all fit and then popped for beer, saltines, and ring bologna afterward.

I thank Susan Lampert Smith, Ron Seely, Anita Clark, Richard Jaeger, Marv Balousek, Dean Mosiman, Rick Barrett, Jennifer Sereno, Jason Stein, and Gena Kittner for not throwing me out of our corner of the newsroom over the years I spent reporting and writing these and other newspaper articles and columns.

I had the best copy editors to work with for most of what is in this book. Not one of them ever pulled a punch: Paul Johnson, Bruce Helland, Marvi Reyes, Julie Shirley, and Nicole Rogers. Any mistakes in here are mine.

I count journalists Dennis McCann and Dennis Chaptman as conspirators in putting the idea for this book into my head, along with journalist-educators Vince Filak and Dan Simmons, whose impeccable timing in asking me to talk about obit writing with their journalism classes at the University of Wisconsin–Oshkosh and Marquette University moved the idea along.

Five women stepped up at moments of doubt to give me a push or snap me into action. Chris DeSmet of the UW Writers Institute steered me in the right direction when it became obvious that for me, fact would always trump fiction. Kate Thompson and Erika Wittekind at the Wisconsin Historical Society Press were way more fun than I expected and more patient than I deserved. A special thank you to Connie Lovett for the writing cubby, warm welcome, and dog-friendly chair in your design studio. Thank you to Julie Overman for reality checks.

Thank you to Dennis McCormick, ace librarian and archivist, persistent in the search for the arcane and, with Chris Lay, so helpful in flagging possible images and forgotten columns.

Likewise, thank you for the above-and-beyond help in finding photographs from Dick Geier, Diane Maida, Catherine Arneson, Kevin Schmidt, and Robert Rahn.

Writing about dead people is a curious job, but a kinship develops once sources know you can be trusted. Over forty-five years, there were lots of them. They were cops, coroners, funeral home directors, investigators, photographers, deputies, doctors, lawyers, social workers, dispatchers, friends of friends, homeless people, beat reporters, librarians, and, always, somebody who knows somebody who might know somebody. Thanks to you all for answering the phone, coming to the door, giving me directions, and letting me listen. I never took you for granted.

To my mom, Alice R. Hesselberg, thank you for always giving writing a special place.

Thanks to Else Karlsen, friend and beloved, a skeptic forever, and our boys, Espen and Eivind, for being curious and not afraid to ask questions. That's where everything starts.

Index

About the Author

George Hesselberg was a reporter for the
Wisconsin State Journal for forty-three
years. He covered every beat, wrote hundreds of news obituaries of the famous and
the not-so-famous, and was a columnist
for eighteen years. In addition to his long
career in journalism, he has worked in
Wisconsin as a cheesemaker, stagehand,
gravedigger, sign painter, and barn roofer.

PHOTO BY ELSE KARLSEN

He has published two books of stories for children, a collection of
articles written at the 1994 Winter Olympics in Norway, and a
collection of columns.

A native of Bangor, Wisconsin, Hesselberg graduated from
the University of Wisconsin–Madison and studied philosophy,
logic, and language at the University of Oslo. In Norway he
worked as a translator, night watchman at the telephone company,
and bartender.